trade show samurai

trade show samurai

The Four Core Arts for Capturing Leads

Mike Moyer

Lake
Shark

Published by Mako Publishing
Lake Forest, IL
www.MakoPublishing.com

To Anne, Anson and Merrily

My Promise

If, after reading this book, you don't feel that it contains not just good advice, but the greatest trade show advice you have ever received in your entire career, I will happily refund your money and apologize for wasting your time.

Mike@TradeShowSamurai.com

Preface

I remember the first trade show I ever attended. It was Mac World at the Bayside Expo Center in Boston. I was 14 years old and I was amazed at all the cool stuff. There were guys showing off their souped-up Apple II computers that had been upgraded with as much as 50 kilobytes of RAM.

I can still remember watching in fascination as dot-matrix printers printed detailed pictures of dragons in black ribbon ink. I'll never forget my introduction to the 3.5-inch floppy disk that held a whopping 1.4 megabytes of data. I never dreamed that I would ever have files large enough to fill such media. It was nothing short of spectacular.

I attended other shows at the Bayside Expo Center. At the Dog Show I brought home beautifully-packaged cartons of Eukanuba dog food. Such premium products—for free! I carefully protected them from our dog lest he eat them and deprive me of their glory.

At the ski show I bought my first pair of skis. At the electronics show I salivated over car stereos. I brought home bags of samples, scores of tchotchkes, and dozens of brochures and catalogs.

Exhibitors handed these items to me without hesitation in spite of the fact that I was clearly a child and the odds that their respective companies were going to be receiving my patronage in the short or medium-term were slim.

In college I had a t-shirt company. I coordinated my trips home so I could stop at trade shows. One year I stopped in Memphis and attended a Screen-Printing Convention. It changed my life. I found new ideas, new suppliers and new business connections that allowed me to bypass the middlemen and increase my profits. I stopped at the Advertising Specialty Conference in St. Louis and had my eyes opened to new possibilities. Shortly thereafter I started selling the very tchotchkes that I had grown to love: little mirrors with company logos, squeeze balls, buttons and coffee mugs.

During graduate school I attended Direct Marketing conventions. I was a direct marketing student at Northwestern and I felt like the entire conference was designed specifically for me. I hung on every word uttered by the speakers, I spent time at every booth and collected reams of brochures and a back-breaking bag filled with trinkets.

I once attended the All Candy Expo at Navy Pier in Chicago. Every major confectionary and snack company was passing out samples like crazy. I had more candy and junk food than I could carry. It was like the ultimate Halloween. I ate candy, I gave candy to friends, I handed candy to strangers, I even tossed candy in the trash.

The Midwinter Meeting in Chicago is the Dental Industry's Mecca. Wait in line long enough (over an hour) and receive a $100 Sonicare electric toothbrush. That is, of course, if you are wearing the badge that indicates that you are a dentist. After 20 minutes at the Midwinter Meeting you will be stocked up with enough tooth brushes, floss and toothpaste to last ten years.

Before long I was speaking at conferences. This was an honor. I spoke at technology and marketing conferences. I held sessions about Customer Relationship Management (CRM), direct marketing and I even did seminars about getting into college. It always felt great to be a speaker. It was like being a mini-celebrity, the kind that people want to meet, but don't want an autograph.

Eventually, I found myself on the other side of the table. In addition to attending trade shows and speaking at them, my employment put me in a charge of actually exhibiting at trade shows. In this role I saw a different side of the equation. On the exhibitor side there is pressure to generate a good return on investment.

By the time I began leading trade show efforts as an exhibitor the Internet bubble had burst and the conference world was taking a massive hit. People were pulling out of shows left and right and those who were still in the business were shrinking their investments.

The problem is that assessing the true value of a trade show effort difficult and trade shows are a major expense. In many cases trade shows are the single largest marketing investment a company makes in terms of both money and time.

For the most part, the results of trade shows are nebulous. A "great" show often means that a show was busy or people had fun. It rarely means a specific number of concrete leads or sales.

I was convinced that these glorious gatherings of business people had value, but because show expenses touch so many different departments it is often difficult to capture the real cost of a show. Likewise, because it was difficult to trace sales to shows it was also difficult to trace revenue to shows. In my search for answers I found a lot of experts in organizing shows, but few of them could really show how to boost return on investment (ROI).

So, I set off to create a system for capturing and tracking leads from a trade show so I could show the true value to the organization. And, under pressure to perform, I was forced to do it with a lot less money. I knew that "good" wasn't going to cut it. It had to be amazing.

I needed a system that looked more like an assembly line than a sales meeting. In needed structure and discipline. It also needed some sort of evidence that it was working.

The system I created was the birth of the Trade Show Samurai.

The first show that I applied the Trade Show Samurai concept to was a huge success. I cut the budget by 80% and captured over 700 leads. In the prior ten years of doing the show the company couldn't point to even one lead that was generated.

I knew I had created something special that would boost ROI to amazing heights. I continued to refine the process. Several years later I created an exhibit that defied even our loftiest expectations. Eight trained Trade Show Samurai captured thousands of leads at a show where our booth neighbors captured virtually nothing. The guy next to us left the show with *twelve* leads.

I had attained what I now realize was Trade Show Nirvana.

The pages that follow outline a key part of my trade show model—the Four Core Arts. These critical skills address how an individual should behave in the booth to capture a crazy number of leads.

At the end of the day it's the behavior of the staff that will make or break your trade show effort no matter how much you have invested in the booth or marketing.

No matter who you are or how good you are at trade shows, I believe these skills will boost your ROI to new heights.

In my experience there is no other communications model—in all of marketing—that can deliver such exceptional results for so little investment.

Welcome to your training to become a Trade Show Samurai. I sincerely hope that once you master these skills you will never go back to you old ways of settling for less than what is possible.

Contents

Introduction

The Trade Show Samurai Arts are a set of skills designed for one thing—capturing leads at a trade show. Apply them properly and you will capture more leads than you ever thought possible (Trade Show Nirvana). Apply them improperly (or not at all) and you will live the life of a mediocre trade show staffer—a pitiful existence if your one goal in life is to collect trade show leads. For most of us, this is not the case. But, why not be good at it anyway?

The four core arts that are discussed in this book are:

1. The Art of Engagement
2. The Art of Intrigue
3. The Art of Inquiry
4. The Art of Disengagement

The Arts are easy to learn, but they take practice to master. They are also difficult in the sense that they will force you to step out of your comfort zone and you may receive pushback from your peers and, in extreme cases, you may be ridiculed by your jealous competition. In the end, however, those who persevere will succeed gloriously.

If you succumb to the existing standards of practice you will continue to experience existing standards of success. These standards seem to be "good enough" for most people, but most people don't realize how much is left on the table at the end of the trade show. They leave satisfied because they never knew what was possible.

What's cool about the Trade Show Samurai Arts is that they are essentially free because they are mostly just honed communication skills that anyone can learn. The ROI is virtually limitless. I will gladly take the "Pepsi Challenge" with any other trade show marketing technique— no matter how fancy, creative or expensive—because I know that the Trade Show Samurai Arts will beat them all in terms of ROI.

The Arts and AIDA

If you've ever been in sales you understand, or at least you should understand, "AIDA." AIDA stands for Attention, Interest, Decision, and Action. This is the backbone of any good sales strategy and it is the backbone of the Trade Show Samurai plan of attack. Here are the basic elements:

1. Attention- how do you get someone to stop in their tracks and give you their undivided attention?

2. Interest- how can you make sure you are delivering a clear, concise message that is of interest to them?

3. Decision- how can you make them decide that you are worth voting for, buying from, or speaking with?

4. Action- how can you get them to take action on their decision as soon as possible? Preferably right now?

Learning the techniques for AIDA in this book will put you well on your way to Trade Show Nirvana.

This is a book about how you can help your company turn trade shows into one of the single most productive marketing tactics they have ever known.

This is *not* a book about organizing trade show exhibits. There are lots of books about that and there are lots of people around who are quite good at that. Getting a fancy trade show booth together, ordering some logo-shirts, coordinating travel, handling logistics, and tipping union employees to go to the top of the delivery list are all fairly well-documented activities.

What is *not* very well-documented is what you are actually supposed to *do* at the trade show.

Ask yourself this: how much time have I spent *training* for how I should act in the booth *before* the actual day of the event? The answer is probably very little, if any at all.

If a company does any sort of training at all, it's usually held in the morning on the first day of the show. They tell all the booth staff (usually the sales team) to meet an hour before the exhibit hall opens so they can go over a few "key messages," go over some new products, or how the spin-to-win game is going to work. Most people come late and miss part of it.

At a trade show, magic happens on the show floor when diligent booth staffers properly engage prospects. They ask questions that will determine whether there is a good fit between the prospect's needs and what the business has to offer. They carefully record the needs of the prospect before sending the prospect on his or her merry way. Unfortunately, this doesn't really seem to happen very often.

More often, hours of organizing and thousands of dollars are spent for naught as the booth staff mill around their exhibits waiting to be showered with attention from eager buyers. They wait and wait. They drink coffee, chit-chat with one another and pass out tchotchkes. Productivity is abysmal.

There is a better way.

It is now time to learn the skills that will transform you and your fellow booth-staffers into a lead-generating machine, the likes of which have rarely been witnessed on the face of the earth.

The first step is to rethink what you know about trade shows.

Visit the Virtual Dojo at TradeShowSamurai.com to access a video seminar about the Trade Show Samurai.

The Trade Show Samurai in Action

Chapter One

the Trade Show Samurai Perspective

In order to master the skills of a Trade Show Samurai you have to ask some very fundamental questions. For instance:

Why do people attend trade shows?

Most people will give an answer like "to see what's new, look for new vendors, get new ideas" and things along those lines. They are mostly right. After all, these are all great things. With this in mind, exhibitors all show up hoping to capture some of the attendees' interest with a well-intentioned inventory of trinkets and $10 brochures. Or perhaps they want to lure them in with a game, a cappuccino bar, or a scantily-clad female from the local talent agency. Again, all great things, lots of fun, and maybe, just maybe, the attendee will stick around long enough to hear your sales pitch.

And, while it may be true that an attendee is there to listen and learn and soak up all that is new and exciting in the industry, there is another, more fundamental, question:

Why does *your* company *exhibit* at trade shows?

Most people will give an answer like "to see what's new, look for new clients, get new ideas," and things along those lines. Take note that these are similar goals as the attendee. They are *learning* goals. Ultimately, like attendees, exhibitors want to learn.

However, nearly all trade show exhibits on the planet are designed to *teach*, not to learn.

This brings me to the essential Trade Show Samurai Perspective. You must adopt this point-of-view if you are to be successful:

The most important job of the Trade Show Samurai is to learn, not to teach.

Let me say it another way:

What you learn about the attendees is far *more important than what they learn about you.*

Looking at the show from this perspective, I hope, will be a real eye opener for you and your coworkers. It is a perspective that turns the game upside down.

At the end of the day, it is your job to learn just enough information about each and every attendee at the show that you can pass them off as a qualifiable[1] lead to your sales department. At any given show there could be thousands of attendees. If you are at the right show a *huge* percent of them are very solid prospects. In fact, there are no other business situations where you have so many like-minded people in so little space.

There is only thing standing between you and all the leads you can handle: time.

---

[1] More later on what a qualifiable lead actually is.

Chapter Two

Know Thine Enemy

By concentrating on *learning* about attendees instead of *teaching* attendees you are actually doing both of you a favor. Trade shows are a veritable sensory overload. It is nearly impossible to take it all in. At some of the larger shows most attendees are doing well if they can just walk every aisle. Most of them are attending seminars as well, so time is very limited. The more time they spend chewing the fat with you or your fellow booth staffers, the less time they have to get around the show. With the right questions, you can determine if the attendee is a good fit with what your business has to offer. If there is a fit there will be plenty of time for them to talk later with the sales department; if there is not a fit you can send them on their way. Either way, you are saving them, and yourself, precious time on the show floor.

One of the biggest mistakes you can make at a trade show is spending too much time with one attendee. In order to capture super-samurai volumes of good leads you have to take advantage of every second at a trade show. There is no such thing as "long hours" on the trade show floor. I don't care how sore your feet are, the time is always too short.

From the moment you set foot through the door the clock is ticking. For the Trade Show Samurais, this is a formidable enemy. Unless you are well trained it will crush you.

Trade show attendees will stream by your booth throughout the show, sometimes steadily and sometimes erratically. Every minute and every second you spend talking to one attendee is time away from others. You must engage and disengage with surgical precision.

Sometimes I hear people complain about "low traffic". Traffic is a time problem; it is not a numbers problem. There are still probably more attendees than you can handle, but low traffic wastes time. You will have to learn how to mitigate the damage caused by slow traffic. You will do this by being "always on." You will engage and disengage on the show floor, at breakfast, at the party, on the shuttle bus, and even on the airplane. I once got my best lead while waiting to get on my airplane after the show was over.

The Trade Show Samurai Mindset

Your race begins when you leave your house to travel to the trade show. *It's on.* Your job is to become a sponge that soaks up professional information from complete strangers. Once you have what you need you should stop the conversation and move onto the next person. You will not be afforded the luxury of long conversations. If your objective is to generate leads then don't try to sell (however tempting). Your selling efforts will waste time.

You do not show product demos, you do not talk about the weather, you do not host silly putting games, you do not drink coffee, you do not take long breaks, and you do not talk to your co-workers. You stand, poised and ready to strike, with your lead-gathering tools close at hand.

Keep this mindset in everything you do. Trade shows are a pressure-cooker of activity.

The Way of the Trade Show Samurai

I know what you are thinking: the mere *suggestion* that you should not be selling every attendee that walks into your booth or showing product demos to every passer-by seems absolutely insane.

Throughout this book I will introduce concepts that may sound petty or illogical at first. This is because you may be looking at the concept from the perspective of a *typical* trade show exhibitor or a *typical* trade show attendee. The Trade Show Samurai is neither.

The Trade Show Samurai does not follow the beaten path to trade show mediocrity; they follow the unbeaten path to trade show extraordinary.

For example, consider a small bowl of mini candy bars sitting on the counter of a trade show booth. I personally love mini candy bars and, as a trade show attendee, I even keep an eye out for them. When I see them I quietly make my way over to them and help myself, being careful to avoid eye contact so I won't have to speak to the exhibitors. It's not that whatever their offering isn't of value to me, it's just that my goal is to get, and consume, a mini *Butterfinger* bar, not to enter a long conversation. Based on my observations at trade shows I see that there are a lot of people who slip into booths just to grab a mini candy bar. My conclusion is that a bowl of mini candy bars gets high marks from the typical attendee.

Most exhibitors I know like the small bowl of mini candy bars too. They can consume them freely throughout the day with little or no guilt because they figure they're burning off the calories anyway. And they see that mini candy bars are also an effective lure for attendees. Sometimes they can intercept an attendee as they are taking one. Sometimes the two of them can consume them together while discussing their favorite flavors. Based on my observations at trade shows, I see that there are a lot of exhibitors who enjoy having a bowl of mini candy bars. My conclusion is that a bowl of mini candy bars gets high marks from the *typical* exhibitor.

The typical, well-beaten path to trade show mediocrity is lined with small bowls of mini candy bars.

But this is not the way of the Trade Show Samurai. The Trade Show Samurai sees a small bowl of mini candy bars as an impediment to getting the job done. She sees it as disrespectful to herself and to attendees. First of all, it is a distraction. Second of all, it wastes time. Third of all, it creates a mess which must be cleaned up (which is both a distraction and a waste of time) Fourth of all, it is wholly unnecessary to the productivity of the trade show environment.

While a small bowl of mini candy bars may seem entirely appropriate and even beneficial to typical trade show attendees and exhibitors alike. It is a detrimental addition to the Samurai-style strategy and would never be allowed by a Trade Show Samurai[2].

As you consider your own Samurai-style strategy, don't use conventional wisdom; think like a Trade Show Samurai.

Visit the *Virtual Dojo* at TradeShowSamurai.com to order a mini candy bar- Free!

---

[2] *The Battle of the Small Bowl of Mini Candy Bars* is often fought by Trade Show Samurais. Sadly, they sometimes lose this battle but survive to fight the greater fight.

Chapter Three

Honor Sales

Without sales, business is nothing. Sales are the point of all business activities. The Trade Show Samurai must honor sales and, with it, the Sales department.

I believe that Sales is part of the overall marketing function and the job of a marketing department is to not only generate sales leads, but also to push them as far down the sales process as possible before a human has to actually get involved. When marketing does its job, sales should be easy(er).

There are two possible objectives for a trade show. The first is to generate actual sales. The second is to generate qualifiable leads that can then be turned into actual sales by a professional sales person. You must decide, in advance, the objective of the show you are attending.

A Magazine with a Pulse

Magazines have articles and ads. So do trade shows. The exhibits are the ads and the seminars and sessions are the articles. Trade shows are essentially giant magazines with a pulse. In fact, they are so similar to magazines that magazine companies are often trade show organizers as well.

You should expect to accomplish the same thing with a trade show as you might expect to accomplish with a magazine ad. The difference is that you can actually reach out and grab your "reader" by the throat if you want to.

So, if your company is the kind of company that makes products and services that can actually be sold through a magazine ad you should expect the objective of your trade show effort to be actual sales.

On the other hand, if your company makes products or services that require the assistance of a professional salesperson to make the sale, the objective of your trade show effort should be to generate qualifiable leads.

Not all trade shows actually allow you to make sales from your booth. The shows that do allow this have a large number of companies that sell products or services that can be sold more or less on impulse. For instance, the Midwinter Meeting for the dental industry has lots of companies that make toothbrushes or latex gloves or small toys for kids. These are the kinds of things that could actually be sold through a magazine ad. A dentist would see the ad and simply pick up the phone and place an order. Accordingly, there are lots of dentists who buy lots of toothbrushes, toys and gloves on the spot at the Midwinter Meeting.

Financial data services, on the other hand, are not impulse purchases and cannot easily be sold through a magazine ad. Like a good magazine ad, a good trade show strategy should motivate the attendee (the "reader") to request more information from a sales person.

Qualifiable Leads

As a Trade Show Samurai, you must understand whether you are trying to drive leads or drive the on-site sale of products. It is your sworn duty to honor sales and let your actions be guided by the ultimate pursuit of sales.

In most business-to-business trade shows, lead generation is the primary objective, but the Trade Show Samurai can use his or her skills for either purpose. However, this book will assume that your Samuraic[3] duty is to generate leads that will then be distributed to the sales department.

In order to properly honor the Sales department, you must be respectful of their time. A salesperson should dedicate the majority of his or her time to high-potential prospects. This means it

---

[3] I know this isn't a real word, I just thought it sounded funny. It's my book and I'll make up words for fun if I want to.

is your job to deliver a lead that can be cultivated into a sale as quickly as possible. For this you will need to deliver *qualifiable* leads.

Most of the time we use the term "Qualified Lead" to loosely imply that the person is in a position to buy your product or service. They need it or want it or have the money to pay for it or have to have it for some reason.

At any given show there are a certain number of possible qualified leads. You won't know who they are unless you talk to them. Therefore, it will be your job to talk to as many people as possible. The more people you speak to, the more qualified leads you will capture.

The sales team will ultimately define what a qualified lead is; "qualifiable" merely means that they will be able to determine if it is qualified and assign the right prioritization to it.

This is important because your ability to rank leads in order of relative importance is going to be appreciated by your sales team. It is much better to hand over a stack of leads with the best leads on top than to simply hand over a random stack of names and addresses.

A qualifiable lead includes contact information as well as a set of data that will help determine if the contact is a good prospect. Pretend you are a new manufacturer of gardening supplies; which of the following leads would you most like to have?

1. Joe Smith, 847-555-4543
2. Sally Jones, 847-555-8739
3. John Doe, 847-555-6847
4. Millie Foley, Mow, Inc., 847-555-5463

Were you able to pick one? Maybe you like working with women better than men so you picked someone with a woman-sounding name. Maybe you figure the one with the company name looks like a better deal. Or maybe you can't really tell. You can always call them all. This is fine if you have four leads, but what if you have 400?

None of these leads are qualifiable. Qualifiable leads have additional information that will help you prioritize them. Here are the same leads, only this time they are qualifiable:

5. Joe Smith, 847-555-4543, janitor at the conference center.
6. Sally Jones, senior buyer for a national garden supply retailer. Looking for new product ideas, $5,000,000 annual budget. 847-555-8739
7. John Doe, lead groundskeeper for Cascade Country Club, 108 holes, ten full-time employees, unhappy with their current supplier, 847-555-6847

8. Millie Foley, Mow, Inc, owner of a landscaping company in your town, two employees, 847-555-8739

These are qualifiable leads. Now which one do you want to call first?

You can clearly see that a qualifiable lead is more valuable than one that is not qualifiable. Most of the time if a trade show exhibitor gets any leads at all they come in the form of a stack of business cards. A business card is not a qualifiable lead. Let me repeat that, a business card is *not* a qualifiable lead.

I don't care how many business cards you collect—they are worthless. To pass off a business card to a member of the Sales department isn't cool. If you think about it, it's kind tacky and disrespectful. Pretend you were handing over a number of someone you wanted the sales person to go out with on a blind date. Would you just hand over the number or would you provide a little background on who the someone is and why you thought they would be a good match?

People pass off business cards all the time, and while it may feel like you are doing them a favor, you are actually creating a lot of busywork that could lead nowhere.

The same goes for show mailing lists, directories and (gasp) contest entries. If all I have is a person's name, title, company name, address, phone number, and email address, I have nothing. I need to add qualifying information.

A qualifiable lead, on the other hand, will allow the salesperson to rank-order his or her list of trade show leads by sales potential. Then they can start their daily calls from the top of the list. If you have done your job right, your Sales team will have the most success with names at the top of the list and the least success with the names at the bottom. This doesn't mean that it isn't impossible to find the gem in the stack of business cards, but finding needles in a haystack is not the best use of a salesperson's time. You need to give them enough information to make good decisions. The faster they can act on a lead, the more revenue you will generate. Remember, as a Trade Show Samurai you are to honor sales and honor the sales department. You will generate lots of leads at a trade show, make sure they are qualifiable. Do not disrespect the Sales person's time.

The problem with trade show leads is rarely quality, but quantity. That's why it's important to be a Trade Show Samurai, because only a Trade Show Samurai can maximize the quantity of leads from a trade show. With a booth full of Trade Show Samurais there is no other marketing tactic that can produce the quality and quantity of leads for the same price. And, while it's true I haven't conducted a scientifically valid study to prove this I would love to have the chance. I'm confident that Trade Show Samurais are the most effective trade show lead-getters hands-down.

Chapter Four

the Art of Engagement

One of the most important and difficult skills a Trade Show Samurai can learn is to properly engage a trade show attendee. It is the *Attention* part of AIDA. Properly engaging an attendee is to secure their attention. Getting their attention will depend on your ability to engage. Keeping their attention will depend on your ability to generate interest.

I visit trade shows all the time. Sometimes just for fun. I request a press pass (I write for some publications as well as my own) and wander the halls to see if I can catch somebody doing it right. It rarely happens. People simply don't know how to engage. No skill is more important. Everything at the show, all the time, money and travel is a total waste if you and your staff can't engage attendees.

People, even talented salespeople, have a natural fear of others. Introducing yourself, cold turkey to a complete stranger is not a skill in which people get much practice. Couple this with the fear of being rejected and you have a recipe for underperformance.

The key to mastering the Art of Engagement is to: one, have a plan and two, practice like crazy.

The plan is simple. You must position yourself properly in the booth, make the right kind of eye contact, and have an opener that works for you.

The Trade Show Samurai Stance

Trade show rules often prohibit exhibitors from soliciting attendees outside the booth. (I've learned this the hard way.) A good Trade Show Samurai will make the rules, whatever they may be, work in their favor. Don't be afraid to bend a few rules. Get the lead, but don't get kicked out.

The proper stance is to face the flow of traffic with one foot on the booth carpet and one foot in the aisle. The line made where the edge of your carpet meets the edge of the aisle carpet is called "Coastline" (more about Coastlines later).

You should never, ever have anything in between you and the attendee. Many people hide behind tables or desks. Trade Show Samurais have no use for these obstacles to success. You will need a wide open-space in which to maneuver. Attendees, who are just as unaccustomed to meeting strangers as you, will naturally try to avoid you. If they start moving away from you, you should be able to casually reposition yourself to intercept.

Keep your hands out of your pockets. Many Trade Show Samurais carry a clipboard or other information-gathering tools in their left hand. A clipboard with paper and pen are important tools even if you have a lead kiosk (more later on this).

Your right hand should be ready for shaking an attendee's hand. If you have sweaty palms you will need find a way to dry them off as much as possible. Try discretely rubbing them against your pant leg. Avoid the clammy handshake.

Choose your mark—find someone in the crowd that you want to speak with. I don't care who it is, but pick them out fast and don't let too many others pass you by. Your job is to speak to every last person at the show so you will eventually talk to the less appealing folks but you will be ready after a few hours of picking the low-hanging fruit.

Most trade show badges are color-coded to indicate the buying role the person has. Blue might be a buyer, green might be a member of the press, red might be a consultant. Once you get your rhythm going you can eyeball the badges to pick the best prospects, but in the beginning choose people who look like the kind of people you can relate to.

Once you have chosen your mark, engage using the "Ten/Five" rule.

The Ten/Five Rule

Several years ago a friend of mine was working as the head of quality at hotel in California. He taught me a very good rule called the "Ten/Five" rule that works very well. It is designed to help hotel staff members be respectful of guests, but it works great for engaging trade show attendees as well.

The rule is that you acknowledge someone when they are *ten* feet away from you and speak when they are *five* feet away from you. If you acknowledge them too soon you have an awkward silence before they are close enough to speak to. If you acknowledge too late you look like you are trying to avoid them but can't. Likewise, if you speak too soon you will be shouting, speak too late and you will startle the other person.

"Ten/Five" strikes the perfect balance.

When you see the attendee approaching the booth, or at least walking in the general direction of your booth, make *gentle* eye contact, smile and give them a little nod. This little gesture breaks the ice and prepares the person to listen to your next comment.

It is important to smile. I cannot stress this enough. Smile, smile, smile, smile, smile, smile, smile. Always smile. Smiles are the primary weapon of the Trade Show Samurai. Things will happen much faster if your smile. I promise.

Now, keep your gentle eye-contact for the next five feet and then speak. It will only take a second for the person to walk five feet into speaking range. Hold the eye contact for your first phrase and then shift your eyes away. Don't stare. Look at their badge and learn their name but, beware, don't assume the name on the badge is their name, they may have borrowed it from someone. Also, avoid calling them by name until you they have introduced themselves. It's creepy.

What to Say

The first thing you say to the attendee will have more impact on your success than anything else. Say the wrong thing and the attendee is gone faster than you can say "buh-bye." Say the right thing and you will be able to slip neatly into the interest-generating phase of AIDA.

What you, the Trade Show Samurai, will say is 90% pre-meditated. You are speaking from a script that you wrote in advance and then rehearsed, rewrote, and re-rehearsed.

Your script will allow you to engage, gather information, and then disengage before the prospect knows what hit them. This is not a time to get to know anyone. You will not be shooting the breeze with the prospect. You will be capturing the information your sales force will need when they follow-up.

Most salespeople will recommend that you always ask "open-ended" questions which force the respondent to provide a more detailed answer rather than yes or no. In contrast to "closed-ended" questions can be answered with a single word, like yes or no. Salespeople are often trained to ask probing, open-ended questions so they can learn more about a prospect and better understand their interests. Trade Show Samurais need to move quicker, they don't have time for too many open-ended questions. Therefore, I recommend asking the right closed-ended questions more often than open-ended questions. I know this is contrary to conventional wisdom.

What you say to your prospect is known as the Battle of Bonsai.

The Battle of Bonsai

Remember, your enemy is time. You must get to the point of the conversation quickly if you are to succeed. The Battle of the Bosai uses a direct, premeditated line of questioning that will allow you to "bucket" your prospect into the right category in the first few seconds. I call it "Bonsai" to keep with the quasi-Japanese theme and I needed a word that implied that your questions use a branching technique like a little tree (get it?)

The correct number of questions to ask is the number that is high enough to provide the information you need to move into your interest-generating stage of the process and low enough not to turn them off. Asking a long series of probing questions can be off-putting.

The Battle of Bonsai is a battle against time. To battle time Bonsai-style ask an introductory question and then base the next question on the answer to the first and so on until you have the information you need. This branching technique will get you where you want to be in just a few simple questions.

Most of the time trade show attendees will fall into a few main categories. Sometimes the categories are "buyers" and "sellers". For instance, if you attend the All Candy Expo you will find that most, not all, of the exhibitors are candy manufacturers. Attendees, therefore, are people who buy from candy manufacturers (like a candy shop owner) and those who sell ingredients to candy manufacturers (like sugar farmers). Sometimes the categories are below you in the sales channel. At a motor home trade show you might find motor home dealers and motor home consumers. At a dental show you might find dentists or hygienists. For whatever reason, there are always two or three dominate types of people. You can and will use this to your advantage.

You will also find competitors, members of the press, and trade show junkies (like me) who may have no immediate value to you. You will need to prepare a message for each type and commit it to memory. In some cases your message will be designed to capture the interest of the attendee, in other cases it will be designed to disengage the attendee so you can move onto the next. I'll cover that process in more detail later. For now you are going to battle Bonsai-style.

You will be armed with a lead card and/or some other type of lead-collection tool. All the answers you hear will allow you to either check a box on the card or jot down a quick note.

The Questions

The first question I like to ask is whether or not they already have a relationship with my company. This works even if you are a start-up and have no customers. It positions you as a contender which, of course, you are (or soon will be).

Let's say I run a manufacturing company that makes candy called "Sugar Lips" and one of their new products, "Tweet Sweets", whistles kind of like "Toot Sweets" from the movie Chitty-Chitty Bang-Bang[4]. Here is how the conversation might go if I was exhibiting at a candy conference:

Do you carry Sugar Lips products?

This is a good opening question because it will tell you if the prospect is worth spending more time with and it is the kind of question that will force the person to lie if they are trying to avoid you which is unpleasant. For example, if they answer "Yes" and they are lying they will have to endure the shame of lying. You will have about two seconds to get them interested. If you blow it (and you will from time to time) you may not get another chance with that attendee. But, don't sweat it, there are plenty more where that came from!

---

[4] Yes, I have kids, Anson and Merrily

My next question is the next branch of the Bonsai tree. I ask it *regardless* of their answer to the first question although I record both answers.

Are you with a retailer or a wholesaler?

In this example, I take advantage of the two- or three-category concept. This question gets them talking about themselves beyond a yes or no answer. If they are one or the other they will tell you. If they are something else they will tell you as well. Sometimes you can tell from the color of their badge what category they fall into and you won't have to ask, you can just say something like, "it looks like you are a retailer- right?" Always confirm, never assume.

Getting critical information like this will help me understand which sales pitch to deliver. I will have memorized a few different options. If I gave the same pitch to everyone I would lose a lot of interest.

My next question will get them talking a little about themselves so the conversation won't seem too one-sided.

What type of products do you specialize in?

This is a nice, open-ended question because it gets the person talking about themselves (which people like) and it will give you an idea how well your product fits in. Penny candy shops may be a shoo-in, but an ice-cream shop may be much harder to close. This question can be answered fairly quickly by most attendees so it works well.

If they told me they don't carry my products already I ask:

Have you heard of Sugar Lips?

This is a closed question which is a good follow-up to open-ended questions because it keeps me in control of the conversation. I don't want another open-ended question because I want to solidify interest in the product. Too many open-ended questions are bad. I'm checking boxes on my lead card. I want to avoid taking too many notes.

If they say "No" to this question you can move into your spiel about the company. If they say "Yes" you can tell them about some new products you are offering in the current customer pitch.

Now that you have them in your booth answering questions it is time to sink your Hook.

Hooks

A "Hook" is a short blurb about your business that is designed to solidify their interest in what you have to say. It is short—a one-liner. It has to focus on one specific part of your business that will interest them. For Sugar Lips, I might use a hook like this:

We have a new candy that can play Vivaldi!

It doesn't matter that Sugar Lips makes hundreds of other products or that it was voted one of the best places to work for in America or that it has been in business for over 100 years. Pick you most compelling hook and stick with it.

Everyone should find your hook interesting no matter what their point of view.

One of the best hooks I've ever used was:

We make a light bulb that cleans the air.

This hook would literally stop people dead in their tracks (even the buyer from Wal-Mart stopped.) It didn't matter that the company made water filters and air filters. All that mattered is that we say something that will secure the interest in the company.

Drawing Them In

By the time I sink my Hook I will have captured their attention. They are now standing near me and I have drawn them into the booth. At first, I held the engagement stance with one foot in and one foot out long enough for them to get within a few feet. As they took a step towards me I *stepped back* into the booth. They step forward, I step back, they step forward, I step back. The key is to give them room to get off the aisle and in your booth. This is important because it's awkward to talk to someone standing in the aisle.

I can also steer someone to a lead-capture kiosk I can enter data as I speak with them.

The *Battle of Bonsai* is very fast. Here is how it might look in action:

The Scene	You are a Trade Show Samurai and have properly engaged a prospect using the Ten/Five Rule	Feet straddle the Coastline
Trade Show Samurai	Hello, do you carry Sugar Lips products?	Hold position on the Coastline
Attendee	No.	Hold position on the Coastline

Trade Show Samurai	Are you with a retailer or a wholesaler?	Take a step backward into the booth (move when you talk)
Attendee	I'm with a retailer.	Pause
Trade Show Samurai	What type of products do you specialize in?	Take a step backward into the booth
Attendee	We carry party supplies, mostly for children's parties.	Pause
Trade Show Samurai	Have you heard of Sugar Lips?	Take a step backward into the booth
Attendee	No, I haven't	Pause
Trade Show Samurai	We have a new candy that can play Vivaldi!	Dramatic look
Attendee	*Thinks: Holy Schneiky! This could be the product that makes my business explode and earns me the respect of my peers!*	Pause

Once you have captured their attention you are now almost ready for the Art of Intrigue. But first…

What *Not* To Say

As important as it is to say the right things, it is equally as important to not say the wrong things. Unfortunately, what comes naturally for people to say is often exactly what they should not be saying.

The following questions and phrases are off-limits for the Trade Show Samurai:

Hello! (Or hi, howdy, ciao or any variation thereof.)

There is nothing simpler to avoid for an attendee than a simple greeting. Dismiss the pleasantries and get down to business.

Can I answer any questions for you?

The point is not for you to answer questions; the point is for you to ask questions. Remember, you are there to learn about them first and foremost.

Can I help you?

Help them do what?? Silly question.

Would you like one of our brochures (or tchotchkes?)

These items are used later in the conversation. Don't blow it by handing them out first.

Are you having a good show?

This question really misses the point of your entire trade show existence.

Stick to the Trade Show Samurai techniques. They are very specific because they work. It's okay to slip up from time to time, but the best Trade Show Samurais will avoid saying these things.

Advanced Techniques: Currents and Cliffs

A "Current" is when there is a big crowd of fast moving people flowing through the aisle. This often occurs right before lunch or when a session is about to begin. Members of the crowd walk quickly and avoid eye contact at all costs. Even people who would otherwise like to stop and speak with you risk getting sucked down the aisle by the Current.

A "Cliff" is the point at which you will not be able to engage an attendee because they have walked past your booth, out of range. The Cliff is approximately ten feet from the corner of your booth. When they go off the Cliff, they are gone.

As effective as the Ten/Five Rule is, it doesn't always work when there is a Current along the Coastline of your booth. You have to engage attendees before they get swept off the Cliff by the Current.

Fighting a Current is a more advanced skill of the Trade Show Samurai and takes a little practice and a nice set of brass balls (if you have them.) The Battle of Bonsai is critical to fighting a Current. You must be on your toes and ask the questions perfectly. Attendees in the Current *will not stop moving* or make eye contact unless you say the right things at the right time, so the Ten/Five Rule no longer applies.

The key to getting someone to stop and talk to you is to go through the Battle of Bonsai perfectly and quickly. You don't have to make eye contact; they just have to be close enough to hear you. Think about this as the "Seven Rule" instead of the Ten/Five Rule. Speak at seven feet and walk with them down the Coastline of your booth. Your success will have a lot to do with the amount of Coastline you have. A ten-foot booth is at a disadvantage because you will only be able to get one or two questions in before they fall off the Cliff. Twenty feet is better because you can go through the whole Battle of Bonsai. Longer is better, however, there is a point of diminishing returns. After 20 or 25 feet you should stop chasing the person down the Coastline because it will start to get pretty pathetic. You can either get them or not.

Push too hard and you will become annoying at best and appear to be badgering at worst.

As you progress through your questions the attendee will start slowing down and may actually look at you. When this happens you have got them and you can start drawing them into your booth.

Here is how the conversation might go:

Do you carry Sugar Lips products?

They will answer "Yes" or "No" and they will keep walking. At least you know they heard you. Don't count on eye contact at this point. Walk with them down the Coastline but stay in your booth, do not enter the aisle.

Are you with a retailer or a wholesaler?

Again you will get a quick answer but the attendee may slow down slightly. They will slow down because they will feel rude if they don't. Sometimes people don't mind being rude, don't let it rattle you. Keep going.

What type of products do you specialize in?

Now they will start slowing down and may even make eye contact. They are still moving, but you are beginning to pull them in by slowing down with every step until they stop, then you start backing up into your booth.

Have you heard of Sugar Lips?

Now, you have got them. Asking this question will likely stop them. They will turn and make eye contact. You are ready to move on.

If they keep walking you can make one last-ditch attempt to capture them before they fall off the Cliff by sinking in your hook:

We have a new candy that can play Vivaldi!

If your hook is strong enough it will stop people in their tracks and turn them around.

Don't underestimate the value of fighting the Current. I've pulled back many-a-valuable lead from the edge of the Cliff. Big buyers often move quickly through the show to avoid be accosted. They *will* talk to you. Even Wal-Mart can be stopped. In fact, I recently pulled in a pack of Wal-Mart buyers from the edge of the Cliff. It's possible and it is important.

Fighting the Current takes practice and skill, but it is worth the effort. Don't worry about being intrusive, that is your job and your sworn duty as a Trade Show Samurai. It is okay for you to go after everyone. It's a trade show after all. Attendees *expect* to be spoken too. If they don't want to talk to exhibitors they should stay out of the exhibit hall!

Even if people give you dirty looks, you must persevere. Since birth we have been asked to not to talk to strangers. When a stranger approaches us, we are conditioned to be cautious or even outright defensive. When you get negative reactions don't let it rattle you. You are still doing the right thing. Your actions and behaviors are honest and respectful. You are not being impolite. When people take stock of what you are up to they will appreciate your initiative; they will not think you are crazy.

Currents and Cliffs are prime hunting grounds. At good shows you may always have a Current. Learn to fight it and reap the benefits of a job well done.

Currents separate the Trade Show Samurai from the Trade Show Weenie. They will take all your cunning. Jump right in head first and you will do well.

I promise.

Chapter Five

the Art of Intrigue

Once you have properly engaged the attendee and captured their attention, you are now in the home stretch. Your chances of obtaining a qualifiable lead are very high. But first, they must be intrigued. Practicing the Art of Intrigue will allow you to draw in the attendee so that they understand the value your company has to offer. You are opening their eyes to possibilities they never thought possible.

Your Hook will be the first step of this process. However, once your hook has stopped people in their tracks you need to be able to expand a little to capitalize on their excitement.

Trailers

Movie companies spend millions of dollars each year on movie trailers and then they hire Don LaFontaine[5] to read them. Movie companies know that movies don't sell themselves. They need a captivating snippet that will get people on the hook and instill them with wanting for their film.

[5] Don was the most recognizable movie-trailer voice of our generation (by "our" I mean "my")

Likewise, the Trade Show Samurai knows that companies don't sell themselves either. They, too, need a trailer to help them pique the interest of the attendee. And, just like movie trailers, the Trade Show Samurai produces different trailers for different audiences.

You will be intriguing as long as you follow a structured routine and give a good, pre-rehearsed trailer. The two or three questions during the *Battle of Bonsai* will have supplied you with the information to pick the right trailer. For instance, if I find out the prospect is a retailer I can use my retailer trailer. If I find out they are from a wholesaler I can use my wholesaler trailer. If I find out they are a member of the press I can use my press trailer[6].

The trailer is a 20-30 second description of your business designed to generate just enough information to generate just enough interest in the prospect that they want to learn more. You don't want to give them everything. You always want to leave them wanting more.

For instance, let's say I'm with College Peas, a company that helps kids find the right college. At the show there are different groups of attendees including guidance counselors and college admissions counselors. I engage the attendee and find out that they are a guidance counselor. Here is my trailer:

[6] See the Art of Disengagement

College Peas is a new service that helps students learn about unique college opportunities that they may never have known otherwise. The service is simple: students complete a profile on our site and our consultants match them with real college opportunities for which they are eligible based on their academic achievement, extracurricular activities and internets. If the student is interested in learning more we will share their contact information and profile details with the college. If they are not interested we will keep their profile private. We do not rent or sell lists of student names.

If you register as a guidance counselor you will be able to monitor the activity of your students who use College Peas, see what colleges are interested in them and provide more specific guidance.

The service is free to students, free to high schools & guidance counselors.

I can get you started right now by registering you and setting up a free account. When you get back to your office your counselor kit will be waiting for you.

May I have your first and last name please…?

That's a good trailer. It is short and to the point. It's free and the counselor has the ability to monitor, and touches on some important points that are important to counselors, such as student-controlled privacy, It also promises a free counselor kit. This carefully designed trailer will capture 70%-80% of counselors without further questions.

If they *do* ask further questions you will have pre-rehearsed answers to provide. For instance if the counselor asks, "how do you make money?" I will answer:

> *We are an advertiser-supported site. Like many sites we charge certain pre-screened advertisers to put their messages in front of the student.*
>
> **pause**
>
> *I can register you right now, it only takes a minute and you will receive some more information for you and your students in the mail including a "Behind-the-Scenes" Admissions DVD that helps students understand what happens to their application once it is submitted.*

Boom—question answered as briefly as possible and the counselor is redirected back to the registration process with a little more detail about what they will receive.

You and your team will need to anticipate all possible questions and prepare answers in advance.

Let's say the attendee indicated that they were a college admissions counselor instead. Here is how a trailer for the same company, College Peas, would sound for them:

*College Peas helps students learn about unique
college opportunities that they may never have known
about otherwise. We work with colleges like you to
identify unique educational opportunities on your
campus and the types of students you are trying to
attract. We will find the students you want and tell
them about your college. If they want to learn more
we will share their contact and profile information
with you.*

*I can get you started right now. It only takes a few
minutes.*

This trailer is even better. It is shorter and
even more succinct. Again, it focuses on points
relevant to the attendee like the fact that College
Peas will work with them to identify students.

Let's say the prospect tries to block by
saying something like, "Interesting, but I need to
talk to our dean of admissions before I can sign up
for anything." A question like this indicates that you
are not talking to a decision maker. No problem,
this is your chance to obtain the decision-maker's
name so you can give it to sales. You can say this:

*No problem. Let me take their name and a few
notes and I'll follow-up with them directly with some
more information.*

You not only overcame an obstacle, but also
improved the quality of the lead by including the
name of the person who is in charge.

Here is another example. This time let's pretend we are with a financial data feed company. We'll call it *SuperFeed Technologies*. The attendee has been engaged and we find out that they are the technical person in charge of the trading desk applications. Here is the trailer:

> *SuperFeed Technologies provides a real-time data feed of all major securities markets. We use a proprietary compression technology that enables a 10:1 compression with no loss of data. No other company can do this. This means that even during peak trading volumes your traders will still receive 100% of the data. All other companies drop lower-volume security data at peak times which leaves your traders flying blind.*
>
> *We offer a number of service levels based on your firm's needs. How many traders does your company support?*

This is another good trailer. It is fast, to the point and moves right into a line of questioning that will provide valuable qualifying information.

Trailer Discipline

Being a Trade Show Samurai requires discipline. Your company may have four or more completely different trailers depending on the show's audience. Your entire team must *memorize* all of them word-for-word including the answers to the questions.

I cannot stress this enough. Everyone who will be in the booth must *memorize by heart* every single word. I don't care how long it takes, you must memorize it.

You will also practice and rehearse your trailer for many hours. This will help you hone it to the point where you are comfortable saying it and it makes sense.

The hard part is getting the attendee's attention; don't mess it up by not having a good trailer. From there it will be smooth-sailing as long as you have a good trailer. The lead is yours to lose. Don't take any chances.

Just to reiterate: *memorize* your trailer.

One reason for memorizing your trailer is to ensure that everyone is delivering the same message. If the message isn't working you can all get together at the end of the first day and discuss potential problems. If there are consistent questions you didn't expect you may have to incorporate the information into the trailer. Then you can all skip dinner, go to your room and memorize the new trailer. Hooray!

Don't Get Into It

If your trailer is right you can avoid "getting into it" with prospects. Getting into the details of your business is *murder* for the Trade Show Samurai. In-depth discussions with attendees are major time wasters. Leave the details to the sales department. It is not your job to discuss the company. You are practicing the Art of Intrigue; you want to arouse curiosity, not satiate it.

Conversations at trade shows can easily go off on tangents. The Trade Show Samurai is doing battle with time and understands that by losing focus, he or she is in serious jeopardy of losing the battle.

You may find someone who is really excited about your company and really wants to know more. If that is the case you have found a very good lead. Say something like this:

> *I can tell you have a lot of good questions and that you are eager to move forward. Joe Blank is our top sales contact for your region. He is somewhere here at the show. If you give me your cell phone number I'll ask him to call you when he gets back to the booth. If you can't connect here I'll put your information in front of him first thing Monday morning. How do you spell your last name?*

Done. Move on to the next attendee.

The Purpose of the Trailer

I said earlier that what you learn about attendees is far more important than what they learn about you. If that is true, you might ask, then why do I make a big deal about the trailer which is all about you? The answer is that you must convince the attendee that your company offers sufficient value as to be worth sharing some professional (as opposed to personal) information. During your trailer the attendee is making up their mind whether to keep talking to you or to walk away. The good news is that if you deliver your trailer as rehearsed, your chances of getting all the information you need is pretty much guaranteed.

An attendee rarely says "no" after I deliver a good trailer. This does happen, but probably only once in five hundred attempts. You are far more likely to lose an attendee's attention during the first few seconds of engagement. An attendee will ignore you, avoid you, insult you or lie to you. Engaging an attendee is the hardest part.

Why Salespeople Usually Aren't Trade Show Samurais

I often find that the Trade Show Samurai-style is off-putting to professional sales people who prefer to spend more time with show prospects. They like to have meetings, connect with their peers and do other non-Samurai-like activities. These things are all fine, but they do not wage a good war on time. That is why I am usually reluctant to allow a salesperson to become a member of the trade show booth staff. I would rather they met somewhere outside the booth.

When I'm running the show I only allow trained Trade Show Samurais to work the booth. If the salesperson is willing to learn the ways of the Trade Show Samurai, I am willing to include them. Unfortunately, this is not common. Even a salesperson with good intentions rarely has the time to invest in the training and rehearsal. I always recommend they stay behind and be prepared to start following-up on leads. It's good to have a few of them on hand to meet with large clients or to accept referrals of really eager prospects.

This isn't a knock against salespeople. It is simply recognition of a difference in style that can cause problems for a Samurai-style show strategy.

Decision

AIDA. You have their attention; you have generated their interest, and now they will decide to "register" with you. I like using the word "register" because it sounds official, almost like an honor. It's a good word. I always say, "let me register you and we can send you our information kit." "Kit" is a good word too. It's almost as if you are offering to send them a cool toy or something. Use these words to close the deal. If you find that "register" doesn't work, pick another word or phrase like "let me hook you up with an information kit," or something like that.

Like I said, after you get their attention they are yours. You rarely lose someone during the trailer. People generally have the social wherewithal to allow you to finish what you are saying. Where you will lose them is when they are making up their mind. Some will be on the fence; they may be suspect because your trailer was too smooth (which is okay). They will ask questions.

It's best if they don't ask questions at all. If you are answering a lot of questions, even if you are doing a good job of answering, you are losing your battle against time. You are getting into it with the attendee and you need to cut bait.

If an attendee can't make up their mind whether to register with your company you need to quickly disengage. We will cover this in more detail later. For now, keep in mind that memorizing the trailer and any associated Q&A will help secure the decision to move forward by the attendee. Discipline is everything. Stick to the script and you will succeed.

Chapter Six

the Art of Inquiry

As I mentioned before, a qualifiable lead is one that has enough information that it can be rank-ordered in terms of potential value to the firm. So, in addition to basic contact information, you must ask a series of questions that will allow you to assign a relative value to the lead.

It is not uncommon for a trade show exhibitor to come home from a show with a pocket full of business cards and think of them as leads. They are not. Business cards are worthless because they aren't qualifiable. While it's true that you may be able to sift through them later and look for chicken-scratch notes on the backs of them, for the purposes of the Trade Show Samurai they are total junk.

A business card is merely contact information. It is virtually impossible to assign a value to a business card. I guess if you were intimately familiar with every known company in the industry you could thumb through them and make some educated guesses. But this is very time consuming and the Trade Show Samurai's arch enemy is time.

Business cards do have a role at a trade show because they can save time during the collection of contact information. But, unless they are accompanied by a completed lead card, I recommend you throw them all away. Later, I will show you your business card's role in the Art of Disengagement.

What to Ask

When you inquire, you must ask questions that will allow you to assign a relative value to the lead in terms of future revenue potential. In other words, you want to be able to later qualify the lead as super-hot, ice cold, or something in between.

When you first set out to engage the attendee, you used the Battle of the Bonsai method and asked a series of short questions. This is actually the beginning of the inquiry process, and you have already begun to collect information that will allow you to assign a value.

In the College Peas example the first question you would have asked would have been, "Are you with a high school or a college?" The answer to this question helps determine the potential value of the lead. In this example the company, College Peas, might want to sell advertising services to colleges but not to high schools. Therefore, anyone who says they are with a college is a more valuable lead. It would be wise to let the sales staff know about this important piece of information.

Trade Show Samurais typically collect hundreds, if not thousands[7] of leads at a trade show. In the College Peas example you will most certainly have more than one person who says they are from a college. Therefore, you must ask additional questions that will help you better understand the potential value.

There are a number of qualities about a college that will help you determine its relative potential. For instance, the size of the college could be a factor as well as its status as a public, private or proprietary[8]. The title of the attendee could be important; an admissions counselor has less decision-making power than the dean of admissions, for instance.

Let's say that College Peas is an online marketing service. It would be important to know if the college is currently using online marketing. It doesn't mean that the lead isn't valuable if they don't use it, but all things being equal I'd rather focus my attention on the people who are predisposed to online marketing.

---

[7] Yes, it is possible to collect thousands of qualifiable leads at one show.

[8] A proprietary college is one that operates on a for-profit basis, like DeVry, for instance.

In some cases you can ask about existing solutions. For instance, do they work with one of your competitors?

Some answers will increase their relative value and others will decrease their relative value. Don't make any judgments for now.

The Dream Lead

The enemy, time, is always advancing. The Trade Show Samurai must move quickly. You will need to concentrate on four to eight essential questions.

It is important to work closely with sales to get this right. Speak to them about the company's top customers and work with them to understand the reoccurring characteristics or behavioral patterns the customers share.

In the College Peas example, the ideal customer may be a private college with a student body of between 5,000 and 10,000 students located in a rural setting with a liberal arts focus and a secular heritage. If this is the case then the "Dream Lead" would be from a private, not-for-profit college with a student body of between 5,000 and 10,000 students located in a rural setting with a liberal arts focus and a secular heritage. *Capiche?*

In order to capture the Dream Lead you will need to ask the following questions:

1. Are you from a high school or a college?

2. Are you public or private?

3. (If private) Are you a non-profit college?

4. How many students attend your college?

5. Where are you located?

6. What is your college's primary educational focus?

7. Are you a religious or secular college?

These are *plenty* of questions to ask and plenty to cover a wide range of possible relative values. The key here is to get them in the big buckets handled and worry less about the details.

Keep an Open Mind

Everything goes here. I've worked for companies where men were better prospects than women and in companies where women were better prospects than men. Is it sexist to rank a woman higher than a man when it comes to potential value? Maybe, but who cares? You are a Trade Show Samurai; you honor sales and sales alone. Give them what they need to be successful.

Check the Box

Notice that all of the questions in the above example are "check the box" questions, in that they are relatively short answer or yes/no questions. Some of the questions are phrased as "or" questions with two answers even though there may be others. For instance, question seven asks if they are a religious or secular college. The college could be a military college. If so, the attendee will tell you even though you didn't mention it. This subtle point is important and will be covered in more detail in the chapter about data collection. The reason the Trade Show Samurai asks questions in this format is because it is fast. Listing out all possible answers is slow.

If you have ever done a telephone survey you will know what I mean. You get questions like this from the surveyor:

> *This question deals with the size of your student body. Answer "A" if your student body is "very small" with fewer than 1,000 students. Answer "B" if your student body is "small" with between 1,001 and 5,000 students. Answer "C" if your student body is "medium" with between 5,001 and 10,000 students. Answer "D" if your student body is "large" with between 10,000 and 20,000 students. Answer "E" if your student body is "very large" with over 20,000 students.*

That is the long way of asking "How many students attend your college?" On your lead card you can check the corresponding box. Do not treat your conversation like a survey or ask questions like a survey.

All questions should have a list of possible answers that the Trade Show Samurai can simply check-off. Open-ended questions take more time and generate a lot of notes which are difficult to manage. Avoid them wherever possible. Use notes, but only use them when absolutely necessary.

Hank, Will and Carl

During each conversation with each attendee you will get a "feel" for whether they are a serious prospect or not. Even a potential Dream Lead can send signals that they won't be a good customer and even a potentially bad lead could show signs of great interest.

You will need to capture this feeling with your friends Hank, Will and Carl. Hank, Will and Carl are codenames for Hot, Warm and Cold. Use these names, or names like it, when you record your lead data. If someone is looking over your shoulder they may be offended if you mark them Hot, or wonder why you marked them Cold, or disagree with your indication that they are only Warm. This kind of discussion is a huge time waster. If they ask about Hank, Will and Carl you can just say they are guys in sales that might handle your lead.

Time Bandits

Hank, Will and Carl is a tool that can help you, the Trade Show Samurai, battle time. The conversations that Hank, Will and Carl help you avoid are Time Bandits that wait to steal time from you. They are devastating to your productivity.

There are many types of Time Bandits. They are little conversation or tasks that keep you from being productive. They are a misplaced pen, or a missing lead card. They are a tangent conversation or a chatty, but worthless, attendee. You must fight them.

Here is why Time Bandits are so destructive. Let's say you and your fellow Trade Show Samurais spend about 1 minute responding to worthless questions every time you talk to someone. Trade Show Samurais are speaking with 1,000 attendees over a three-day period you will waste 1,000 minutes or over *16 hours* of time. In this same time period you could have spoken to 200 other attendees increasing your productivity by 20%.

Never underestimate the damage of Time Bandits. Look out for them. They are small, seemingly insignificant and easy to overlook.

Total Time Bandits

In many cases the Time Bandit will be an attendee that has no potential value to your sales team. While most of the people visiting your booth will be potential customers, there are many that will *never* be a potential customer. These people include competitors, other exhibitors, and members of the press. You will need a plan to disengage these people quickly and quietly.

These people are Time Bandits not because they aren't sometimes important, but because they don't make good sales leads. Members of the press, for instance, could be very valuable contacts indeed, but if you are a Trade Show Samurai in the heat of battle you will have little time to speak with them. You will have to politely disengage by either passing them off to the designated *Press Ninja* or schedule a time when they can meet with the Press Ninja later. More on Ninjas later…

When Good Prospects Turn Bad

Sometimes a good prospect will turn into a Time Bandit after they have given you the lead details. They like you now and want to chat. You intrigued them and they want to chat. The like your shirt and they want to chat. They, for whatever reason, want to chat, chat, chat, chat, chat! Nooooooo! You must disengage!

Advanced Skills

Chapter Seven

the Art of Disengagement

Just as you needed a strategy for engaging attendees, you also need a strategy to *dis*engage an attendee. The Art of Disengagement is an important one. Poorly done, you can offend an attendee and jeopardize the later sale.

There are two circumstances under which you will want to disengage the attendee. The first is after you have collected the qualifiable lead information and the second is when you recognize them as Time Bandits.

In the first scenario the attendee will be fulfilled having gone through all the necessary steps. You have engaged them, interested them and motivated them to divulge some professional information that will lead to a prosperous future. They are happy that they can move on knowing that you will follow up with them later. It's one less thing they have to worry about. Disengaging an attendee after inquiry is respectful of their time and yours. Standing around chit-chatting about the weather or the party the night before is wasteful and disrespectful.

In the second scenario you will be cutting off someone who may have many questions. This is more difficult. Cut them off too abruptly and you will get a bad reputation. Talk with them too long and you will not only waste time, but also risk divulging information you shouldn't.

The Trade Show Samurai has a special weapon; it is a tool that neatly marks the end of a conversation. Wield it wisely. It's called a Trinket.

The Tao of Trinkets

Trinkets include brochures, business cards, posters, caps, t-shirts, pens with crazy hairdos, flashing buttons, squeeze balls, DVDs, CD ROMs, press kits, candy bars, post-it notes and any other sort of tchotchkes under the sun that an exhibitor brings to a trade show with the intent of passing out to attendees.

Most companies bring these things with the expectation that they will be used to attract or engage attendees. That is why it is so easy to walk out of a trade show with a bag full of toys to take to your kids without speaking with anyone. I've seen trade show staff simply handing Trinkets to people as they walk by. I got a sweet set of Skype headphones that way.

A Trinket is not an engagement tool, it is a disengagement tool.

Whether you like it or not, most Trinkets wind up in the trash can. Walk by any trash receptacle at a trade show and you'll see s fair number of Trinkets in there. Sometimes the Trinket is cute enough to get home to your kids where they will play with it for about three hours before your wife throws it in the trash. Like the stuffed monkey I dragged back from China, it lasted about a day, I think.

I love collecting Trinkets at trade shows. I put them all in one of those Trinket-sacks that some companies pass out. I take it back to my hotel room and toss about half of them into the trash. Then I put the remaining Trinkets in my suitcase being careful to toss out anything that puts my bag over 50 pounds so I won't have to actually pay to get the stuff home. When I get home I give some of the Trinkets to my kids and take the rest of it to my office where it sits on the floor under my desk for about six months before I toss it in the trash. I save the sack and give it to my wife who tells me she will use it for groceries.

I have never been inspired to rush out and buy an enterprise management system because of a Trinket.

This realization is heartbreaking for the company who passes out $10 brochures thinking that every prospect that gets one takes it back to their company and pours over it with their senior staff.

The Trade Show Samurai knows better. In fact, the Trade Show Samurai couldn't care less if the Trinket she passes out winds up in the trash. That's because the moment she gives the Trinket to the attendee it has fulfilled its ultimate and complete purpose: disengagement.

To disengage, the Trade Show Samurai hands the attendee a Trinket and says:

> *"It was really nice meeting you. I'll make sure one of our salespeople follows up with you right after the show. Take this [Trinket], it has our phone number and web addresses on it; if you don't hear from anyone feel free to give us a call."*

This is a nice way to disengage. When you hand someone a Trinket at a trade show it marks the end of the conversation and everybody can move on. It's like magic. However, if you give the Trinket to them at the *beginning* of the conversation it creates an awkward tension, almost embarrassment.

Visit the Virtual Dojo at TradeShowSamurai.com to order a *Free* Trade Show Samurai Trinket! Free stuff! Hooray!

The Non-Samurai Way

In the non-Samurai-style booths conversations are often strained and awkward. This is because so many people think that the Trinket is meant to be given at the *beginning* of the conversation. This may seem like a subtlety, but the impact is significant.

Think about it. Whatever your company does, you exist to create some kind of value for your clients above and beyond what they pay you. I may sell them a financial data feed for a few thousand dollars a month. They can use this data to power their trading desks that allow their traders to make millions. With millions of dollars' worth of value at stake why would you need a pen with a crazy hairdo to attract a prospect? The mere notion of is insulting to you both. A *serious* conversation about a multi-million dollar advertising program does not start with a squeeze ball. It starts with two intelligent businesspeople having a meaningful conversation. That's what the Trade Show Samurai does.

When the Trinket is given at the *end* of the conversation it serves as a small token of respect and gratitude to thank the person for the few minutes of time they spent with you. It does not assume that they would value it over your company's value proposition. A pen with a crazy hairdo would be a nice thank you for five minutes of their time, however.

The same concept applies to putting games, spin-to-win games, booth babes, or any other kind of cheap parlor trick. These things are pathetic attempts for a company to placate their fear of introducing themselves to strangers. They are a crutch for booth staffers.

The other problem with passing out Trinkets or playing silly games at the beginning of the conversation is that the attendee may have really wanted the Trinket or to play the game. In this case they will painfully listen to your trailer because they want to move on and collect more stuff. Don't get me wrong, I love Trinkets as much as the next guy, it is fun to collect it at trade shows. It's like adult Trick-or-Treating. But, the Trade Show Samurai honors sales and battles time. Passing out Trinkets to *attract* attendees degrades both.

I know what you may be thinking. "The mugs we passed out last year were great!" They may be great, but 99% of them were tossed out or left in hotel rooms. It's all the same. Trinkets can and will serve their useful purpose at the end of a conversation. Don't put any more value on it that is due.

Here are a few pointers about buying Trinkets for disengagement:

1. **Business cards are great Trinkets.** Handing someone a business card is a great way to respectfully end a conversation. Don't give them *your* card; give them the

card for your head of sales. After all, you don't want them to call *you*; you want them to call sales (if they keep the card at all)

2. **Make it personal.** When you pass them your sales manager's business card take a pen and write your name on it, then circle the sales managers cell phone and say something like, "feel free to call Tom on his cell phone and tell them you spoke to me, Mike, at the conference." This makes it personal. At one show we had a kiosk application that would allow us to set up an account and assign a password on the spot. We would write their password on a little card and hand it to them. It was a great little Trinket. When they threw it away it wouldn't matter because we would send them an email telling them how to retrieve their password anyway.

3. **Make it relevant.** I once worked for a company that had a name that rhymed with "cap" and a cap was our logo. We passed out real caps that looked like our logo. We bought 20,000 of them for less than two dollars each and used them at dozens of shows. It was cheap, but it was high enough quality that it didn't reflect poorly on our company.

4. **Make it trash-resistant**. All Trinkets eventually wind up in the trash, but sometimes you can give it a little staying power. For instance, if you create a souvenir of the event people will often hang onto it for a while. For example, if you are exhibiting at a show in New York you could pass out a Statue of Liberty souvenir that includes your company logo.

Becoming a master at the Art of Disengagement is one of the most valuable skills a Trade Show Samurai can have. Conversations can spin off on all sorts of time-wasting tangents. Time Bandits will leech valuable information from you and chew through valuable time.

Pitch or Ditch?

During attendee engagement you will learn a few details about the attendee that will help you decide which of your memorized trailers you will deliver. Not everyone will receive a trailer. In some cases you realize that the person you are talking to is a human time bandit and you will have to abort the conversation and disengage the conversation quickly.

In these situations you will have to make a split-second choice with regard to the Time Bandit's potential value to the firm. Many will have no or very low value to the firm. Competitors, other exhibitors who are "bored" so they are wandering the halls, students, expo hall employees looking for free stuff, etc. These Time Bandits have feelings too so as much as you might like to release your Samurai fury, you will have to restrain yourself and use some tact.

This will require all of your cunning. Many of these people will be very interested in picking your brain. Competitors, for instance, would love to know what you are up to. Students want to learn from you and emulate your success. They are inquisitive to say the least. You will have to be firm, but polite as in this example scenario:

The Scene	You are a Trade Show Samurai staffing the booth for Vicarious Communications, Inc. A company that offers marketing services to the veterinary industry. You have assumed the Trade Show Samurai Stance and you have engaged an attendee using the Ten/Five rule. You have no idea they are a time bandit because you can't make out their badge.
Samurai	Hello, have you registered with Vicarious Communications yet?
Time Bandit	No, I haven't.
Samurai	Are you a veterinary office or a product manufacturer?

Time Bandit	Neither, actually, I'm a marketing consultant. I heard about you from one of my clients.
Samurai	*Thinks: Drat! A Time Bandit. She is a consultant, I'm not sure what that means, it could be bad or good. Must investigate. The Trade Show Samurai holds his position at the front of the booth. This leaves the Time Bandit in the aisle where conversation is difficult and uncomfortable.* I hope you heard good things! Which client was it?
Time Bandit	It was one of my pharmaceutical clients. How does Vicarious get its clients?
Samurai	*Thinks: He won't answer my question and instead asked a strategic question. He is trying to pick my Samurai-brain. Abort! This guy is worthless!* We use a number of sales programs like trade shows, for instance. We've had a busy show. We have a lot of information on our site. Here is my card with the web address. Take a look when you get back to the office. Do you have a card I can have?
Time Bandit	Thanks, I have a card here somewhere.

Samurai	*While Time Bandit is searching for his card the Trade Show Samurai moves to engage another attendee under the assumption that the conversation has ended.*

The above example shows a quick and polite disengagement. The Trade Show Samurai uses a couple of very important techniques. First, he held his ground in Trade Show Samurai Stance. In a normal circumstance the Trade Show Samurai would step back into the booth drawing the attendee with him until they are both on the booth carpet, preferably near a data college kiosk. However, faced with a Time Bandit, the Trade Show Samurai leaves the attendee in the aisle. It is tough to carry on a meaningful exchange if you are standing in the aisle.

Notice the Trade Show Samurai asks for the Time Bandit's business card. For some reason trade show attendees are pretty bad about having business cards handy. Many of them keep cards in their wallets or purses. If they happen to have one in their pockets it is usually mixed in with a bunch of other business cards. In most cases it will be a struggle for the Time Bandit to produce one. This will provide just enough time for the Trade Show Samurai to move over a little bit and engage another attendee at which point the Time Bandits efforts have been thwarted and they will slip away.

If the Time Bandit tries to walk around you to enter you booth *stand still.* Make no attempt to follow nor should you discourage the Time Bandit from entering your booth. Instead, let them make the move. This will mean they are no longer face-to-face with you and you will be free to immediately engage another attendee before the Time Bandit even knows what's going on.

If the Time Bandit persists, the Trade Show Samurai can hand him or her a business card. This formally marks the end of the conversation. The key is to have several techniques for avoiding the conversation.

If the Time Bandit approaches another Trade Show Samurai in you booth they will receive the same treatment.

Don't get me wrong. I'm not advocating that you be rude or dismissive to Time Bandits. I'm trying to sell you on the fact that your time is valuable and it should be directed to productive activities. You need a strategy for getting back to work and avoid wasting time.

High-Value Time Bandits

Some Time Bandits may actually have a value to your company. You may come across individuals with high potential as investors, partners, or even future employees. Members of the press, for instance, can be valuable allies. Time Bandits like these are important and should receive the attention they deserve, however, Trade Show Samurais honor sales and these people will not lead directly to a sale.

Sure, a good article can generate leads that may turn into sales, but rarely will a salesperson make a sale to a member of the press. The same goes for investors, partners or employees.

Most Trade Show Samurais will have to stick to the script and will not be trained to deal with these non-sale prospects. In these cases you will have to disengage by redirecting the Time Bandit to a Ninja.

Ninjas

A *Ninja* is a person from your company that is specially trained to deal with non-sales prospects or Valuable Time Bandits. There are different types of Ninjas depending on the need. They are trained to handle special cases. A Ninja may not even be at the show.

Press Ninjas

Press Ninjas are trained to speak with the press. It is good to have at least one Press Ninja at the show because there are usually a lot of journalists there. When faced with a Time Bandit who is a member of the press deliver your Press Trailer that will sound something like this:

Thank you for stopping by, we have some really interesting stories here at NiceBox.org. For instance, we just received a government grant to help fund some of our educational programs. We also signed up ten new fortune-500 sponsors over the past sixty days. Our programs are being run in over 2,000 public and private schools across the US and Canada. Mike Moyer is our primary press contact. I would be happy to introduce you right now.

If the Press Ninja is busy you can make an appointment for a later time. You should have a notebook with the Press Ninja's schedule in a safe place that can be accessed by the Trade Show Samurais should the need arise.

Sales Ninjas

Sales Ninjas are members of your sales staff who will be prepared to spend more time with an attendee than a Trade Show Samurai. I like to invite a few of the top salespeople to be on hand at the show. Not at the booth, necessarily, but at the show. They can set appointments with major clients ahead of time and, if an attendee keeps asking questions after you have attempted to disengage you may need to refer them to a Sales Ninja by saying something like:

It sounds like you have a lot of good questions. Let me grab Sally who can provide additional detail.

(look around). Hmm, Sally isn't here but I'll grab her schedule. Looks like she will be back in the booth at 2:00, shall I pencil you in for a quick meeting?

Investor Ninjas

Investor Ninjas are individuals who are in a position to talk about investment. It is okay if you don't have any investment Ninja's at the show. You can simply collect the individual's contact information on a lead card and stick it in the Investor Ninja's folder. The same process would apply to a Human Resource Ninja.

Presentation or Demo Ninjas

I don't often recommend doing demos or presentations in the booth (I never recommend doing live Internet demos of web software). However, occasionally the demo can solidify interest in a simple product or service. Trade Show Samurais *never* do a demo or a presentation themselves. The Presentation or Demo Ninjas do it.

Other Ninjas

Marketing Ninjas, **Operations Ninjas** and Other Ninjas are people who are in a position to handle questions about company specifics. If a potential marketing partner approaches you at the booth you may want to put them in touch with a

Marketing Ninja. You will have these Ninjas designated and trained before the show and they will be prepared be handle any inquiries.

The primary reason for Ninja's is to allow Trade Show Samurais to disengage and get back to their work of gathering sales leads without losing out on a potentially good contact for your firm.

Trade Show Samurais as Ninjas

Sometimes a Trade Show Samurai has the skills and expertise to be a Ninja. This is quite common. As the president of the company I could be just about any type of Ninja I want. However, Ninja activities are a distraction from the job of a Trade Show Samurai so you must "stay in character". Don't do Ninja stuff when you are in Trade Show Samurai mode and vice-versa. This means that if you are capturing a lead as a Trade Show Samurai you can't just move right into a lengthy presentation. If you do this you will be distracted all day.

Stick to the program and you will be successful.

The Trade Show Ninja

Gifts

Some companies like to bring gifts for good customers. This is useful because it will make someone feel more appreciated when you disengage them. For the average attendee you might disengage them with a business card. For a "good" customer you could have something special. This will help you disengage customers in a very meaningful and respectful way. For instance, I once saw a company who gave a nice bottle of wine to any customer who stopped by the booth.

If you do this you will have to be disciplined about it. If you start passing out gifts willy-nilly to *just anybody* it will have the opposite effect. Even if you come across the most exciting prospect in the world, *do not* give them anything reserved for customers. If the president of the United States stops by don't give him (or her) the customer gift[9]. The gift often gets its value from who you *don't* give it to.

Nimble and Quick

[9] What has he done for you lately???

Trade Show Samurais move quickly. The entire conversation with an attendee should take *less than three* minutes. This is not a lot of time, but it is the right amount of time. Trade Show Samurais do not rush. They take all the time they need and none of the time they don't

The reason the conversations go so quickly is that they are highly scripted, memorized and rehearsed. The Trade Show Samurai carefully controls the conversation from beginning to end.

A conversation with a Trade Show Samurai is meaningful, fulfilling and respectful. The attendee gets just the information they need to make a decision to learn more. The attendee, who is also short on time, can get back to browsing the halls. The conversation is fulfilling because the Trade Show Samurai asked questions about relevant, non-threatening professional topics and the attendee feels as if they had a chance to speak. Additionally, the trailer delivered was highly relevant to their interests.

Too Aggressive

Because conversations move so quickly, one of the most common criticisms of the Trade Show Samurai technique is that it is too aggressive. This critique is often generated by less motivated individuals who don't understand how the process works. All they see is a trade show booth with a *frenzy of activity.*

There is some merit to this criticism, however, because Trade Show Samurais are in a constant battle for time. It is easy to forget to that you are dealing with human beings who deserve to be treated with the utmost respect. These people are the people who will be paying your salary. They are your future customers.

When you are in the heat of battle against time you must maintain your poise and respect for those around you. I, myself, have been lost in my pursuit of leads. It is not uncommon to find yourself being short with people and developing distaste for those who are getting in between you and your goal.

To overcome this important risk, take a moment to *Lock and Reload*.

Lock

At the end of each conversation take a few seconds to "lock" the conversation. Locking the conversation means that you will double-check the data on the lead card and/or in the kiosk. It means jotting down any important notes the sales team will need. And it means mentally reviewing the conversation in your head to make sure it went the way you had planned. This quick little review will not only ensure you have carefully captured the information you want, but also it gives you time to reflect on how you behaved. Were you gentle and kind or were you forceful and rude? If you were the latter, don't worry about it. On the off chance that you did offend someone you have another chance to make it right with the next attendee.

Reload

After locking the conversation take another few seconds to reload. Reloading means to make sure the data is saved and the kiosk screen is reset and ready for the next person. It means tucking the completed lead card to the back of your clipboard or in another safe place. It means making sure you have a clean lead card and another Trinket to dish out to the next person. You will also have a moment of calm for yourself.

During this moment of calm, take a deep breath, make sure you are wearing your best smile and get mentally prepared to go back out there.

When you Lock and Reload you will be towards the interior of the booth. This should buy you the time to get prepared before you assume the trade show stance. When you are ready, step back up to the edge of the booth and do it all over again.

Taking Breaks

If you feel yourself getting short with the attendees or missing your lines or taking too much time, you need to take a step back and relax. Let the other Trade Show Samurais know that you are going to take a break and the leave the booth. Go off to the side, get a drink of water, have a snack. Take just enough time to clear your head and then get back to work. Hour-long coffee and lunch breaks are not for the Trade Show Samurai. They leave the booth, eat lunch and return without wasting a lot of time. Just because you are taking a break, it doesn't mean that time stops.

Huddle

At the end of each day do a huddle with the rest of the Trade Show Samurais. The first order of business will be to collect all the lead cards and give them to the team leader or whoever else is designated to take care of them. This is one of the most important things you will do all day. Protect the leads with your life.

Let me reiterate- *protect the leads*. Download them from the kiosks, email the data back to the office, keep the lead cards in a safe place. The value of the lead cards is equal to the entire value of all the booth equipment.

Again- *protect the leads*.

The next order of business will be to discuss the day and any changes you made to the trailer on the fly. Even though all the Trade Show Samurais memorized the trailer, they will naturally adapt it during the day to make it more comfortable to say and to achieve better results.

Teach each other what you learned throughout the day. This time with the team will be incredibly valuable. Congratulate each other. You had a long day, but it's not over.

At the Party

Inevitably, there are parties and events at trade shows. The Trade Show Samurais see these as additional opportunities to get leads. They pair off and hit the important events with the goal of laying the groundwork for the next day. Trade Show Samurais know that parties are work activities and they are still on the job.

Have a drink, but only one or two. It's okay to have a good time, but nothing can kill a good trade show than a hangover. There will be a time to party, but this isn't it, ironically.

As you and your wingman (or wingwoman) work the room, meet the people that look interesting, be enthusiastic about the show and invite them to the booth. If it feels awkward to do business at a party, I have some good advice: *get over it.*

Bring lead cards with you and work the crowd. Parties at trade shows are *not* social events, they are *business* events. You are on a business trip doing business work. Trade Show Samurais understand this and stay on the ball. People who confuse business parties with real parties wind up face down in the gutter looking like a total ass. This is not you.

This doesn't mean you shouldn't enjoy yourself; business parties are a great way to reenergize and meet new prospects. Enjoy the evening, my fellow Trade Show Samurai, tomorrow is another big day!

Chapter Eight

a Zillion Percent Increase

If you learn the ways of the Trade Show Samurai and master the Arts of Engagement, Intrigue, Inquiry and Disengagement you will achieve results that approach a zillion percent or more.

This is because your practice of the Trade Show Samurai Arts will enable to process attendees in not only a processional and respectful manner, but also as fast as humanly possible.

Nine times out of ten the limitations of a trade show aren't the venue or the booth or the traffic or the economy. The limitation is the failure of trade show booth staff to successfully turn trade show attendees into qualifiable leads. When my band of Trade Show Samurais is operating near Trade Show Nirvana the only limitation is ourselves. If we added *twice* the number of Trade Show Samurais we would have *twice* the number of leads.

Everything you do to organize a trade show merely sets the stage. You are the actors on the stage, how you act determines the success of the show.

Practice, Practice, Practice

When I do a trade show the other Trade Show Samurais and I train for many hours during the weeks and months before the show. Training involves a number of active sessions for the Trade Show Samurai.

During early sessions we review sales trailers. We go over and edit the trailers for each category of attendee as well as a press trailer, investor trailer and potential employee trailer. We critique them and then commit them to memory.

We also brainstorm about possible questions and outline answers for all of them. We write up the answers and, again, we commit them to memory.

Memorizing this material is critical. It all needs to be second nature. We don't want to have to think, we want to act. Adaptations will happen naturally as you actually start talking to attendees, but memorizing is the place to start. Consistency is key.

After we have memorized the trailers we rehearse them aloud in front of each other. We want to make sure the trailer sounds natural and makes sense. We rewrite parts of it if necessary. Everyone practices the trailers and the Q&A until it is perfect.

Next we outline the right questions for engagement. We all work from the same script and it isn't final until we all agree. We are clones of one another. While each of us will develop our own style, we will do it from a common ground. This is not a time for improvisation.

We work closely with the sales department to develop a lead card—*the* essential Trade Show Samurai tool. It helps guide our engagement questions and it helps us understand how the conversation should flow. More about the lead card is coming in a later chapter.

All the Trade Show Samurais practice in front of one another. During role play we try to create every possible situation that might occur at the show. We will continue to tweak and edit the materials. Everyone will re-memorize the changes. We rehearse and rehearse and rehearse until we get it right.

We go over disengagement and practice during role play with varying levels of intensity. For instance, we might do a role-play where we pretend we are an aggressive competitor or hot prospect. This type of practice will help us on the show floor.

Rehearsal

We don't stop there. If possible, we will actually set up our booth and rehearse in a natural setting. We will discuss the location of the booth and the potential traffic patterns. Is the booth near the bathrooms? Will that hurt or help? Where is the coffee shop? Should we try and engage people who are on their way to the bathroom or on the way back? How can we position ourselves to maximize exposure? How will we change position at different times of the day? For instance, in the morning we might want to engage people on the way to the bathroom, after lunch we may want to engage them on their way back.

We will also discuss the arrangement of the booth and how to maximize use of the data collection kiosks—more on this later.

Dress Rehearsal

When we are ready, we will invite others from the organization to role play as attendees and we will do a dress rehearsal. We prepare "situations" for the guests. For example, if we were preparing for the College Peas trade show, we might give them slips of paper that say:

- You are a high school guidance counselor from a large urban public school; you need to go to the bathroom.
- You are an admission counselor from a small, liberal arts college in rural Tennessee, you are excited about everything
- You are a potential investor looking for a deal.
- You are a competitor looking for inside information.
- You are a reporter from the Wall Street Journal, you've heard some bad things about the company's management team
- You are a principle from a mid-size suburban public high school; you are in a great mood

This type of rehearsal really sharpens the Trade Show Samurai's skills. The mock-attendees provide valuable feedback that can be used to further hone the message of provide some direction to a Trade Show Samurai that may be leaving the wrong impression. We incorporate feedback into the trailers and the Q&A and we memorize all over again and do more rehearsal.

One of the primary benefits of exhaustive rehearsal is that it will help build the Trade Show Samurai's confidence. On the show floor confidence is everything. You need it to successfully engage, you need it to successfully navigate the conversation and you need it to successfully disengage. If the Trade Show Samurai is prepared for every situation then the show will go smoothly.

The dress rehearsal should be as authentic as possible. Wear your uniforms[10], this will ensure that it fits and coordinates well with the rest of the team. Use the real booth if possible. If setting up the real booth is impractical, get some masking tape and tape out an outline of the booth on the ground. Test out your kiosk software by setting up some makeshift kiosks if you have to. Make sure everything is working properly. You don't want any surprises on the day of the show.

Visit the Virtual Dojo at TradeShowSamurai.com to download some sample training materials.

---

[10] More later on uniforms...

Practice Makes Perfect

Screwing Up

In spite of all your preparation, you will still make mistakes. It is not uncommon for a budding Trade Show Samurai to start getting really nervous about making mistakes, forgetting their lines and experiencing general stage fright. This is very common. You will screw up. I*t's* going *to happen.* Here is my advice: *don't let it bother you.*

In fact, expect to screw up pretty much every time during the first hour or so of the show. You will engage the lowest number of attendees during this period and you will deliver a lousy trailer to most of them. Who cares? It doesn't matter. What matters is that you keep your head in the game and concentrate on improvement. Think *progress*, not perfection.

Getting over the fear of what might go wrong is very important. Fear is a huge time waster. I once trained a group of women to be Trade Show Samurais. They were veterans of the show and had done it "the old way" for years. They were petrified that taking notes on a lead card would offend people. They came up with every imaginable excuse. I arrived about 30 minutes after the show started to find them sitting on chairs, sipping coffee, and chatting with one another. They looked up at me and informed me that "people really don't like the clipboards." The clip boards and lead cards were tucked out of site. Their fear was a self-fulfilling prophecy. They imagined the worst and looked for things to validate their concern. I took the lead cards back out, assumed the stance, and started working the aisle. By the end of the first day we had collected well over 150 leads.

If you think about it, filling out a lead card and taking notes when speaking with a prospect isn't offensive. What is really offensive is *not* taking notes. This is business, it's not social hour. Business people pay attention and take notes so they can go back to their offices and solve some problems for their clients.

If you can muster the courage you will eventually overcome your fear and will be performing at a fairly consistent pace. It won't take long. On day two of the show you will rock. In fact, you will rock until the end of the show unless you give up early. A real Trade Show Samurai won't stop engaging and pitching until he or she is on their own doorstep.

Being a Trade Show Samurai is very much like being a stage actor. There are scripts, sets, costumes and an audience. The difference is that the show is interactive and performed on a one-on-one basis or for small groups at a time.

As an actor leave your other self behind and immerse yourself into the core arts of the Trade Show Samurai:

The Art of Engagement

- Assume the Trade Show Samurai Stance

- Get the attendee's attention using gentle eye contact and the Ten/Five rule

- Ask a short series of qualifying questions to determine which trailer they will receive

- Sink your hook

The Art of Intrigue

- Step back in to the booth drawing the attendee with you until you are both standing on the booth carpet, out of the aisle

- Deliver your memorized and rehearsed trailer

- Be prepared to answer questions with pre-rehearsed answers

- Move quickly into additional qualifying questions and don't get sucked into the details

The Art of Inquiry

- Ask a series of questions with answers that will allow you to assign a relative value to the lead

- Capture the data

- Control the conversation, but be respectful. Beware of Time Bandits, do not let the attendee take over the conversation

The Art of Disengagement

- When you have all the qualifying data you need the conversation is over

- Mark the end of the conversation with a Trinket

- Redirect valuable Time Bandits to Ninjas

- Disengage other Time Bandits and move quickly to another attendee

- Lock and reload

Becoming a Trade Show Samurai and keeping true to your training will have a positive impact on your trade show effort. Implementing a Samurai-style strategy may be difficult. You will face fierce opposition from others in the company. Build support among senior staff, use this book.

You will prevail and you will come closer to Trade Show Nirvana every time. Even if you only experience glimmers of hope along the path, you will know that you are doing your best and your work is truly remarkable. It is something to be proud of because you are doing the right thing.

The right thing, now that you know these skills, is to use them to the best of your ability. Not using them would be to sell short your employer, your employees and yourself.

This may sound a little overly dramatic, but I do believe that when new knowledge comes available it becomes part of one's responsibility to take advantage of it.

Visit the Virtual Dojo at TradeShowSamurai.com to download the "Dos and Don'ts" Pocket Guide

Chapter Nine

the Art of Familiarity

Everyone likes to see a familiar face in the crowd. It's human nature to find comfort in familiar things. The more chaos and confusion there is, the more important a familiar face becomes.

You may already be a big brand that everybody already knows. Or maybe you have been in the industry so long that you are a legend in your own time. These are all great, but what if your brand is *not* already burned in the minds of every member of the human race?

The Art of Engagement is an excellent technique for getting people to talk to you. However, you are still reaching out to virtual strangers and it's always nice to have something to break the ice. Nothing can break the ice faster than a familiar face.

But, how do you become familiar if you are a new company or a largely unknown company or if you are part of the other 90%+ companies who most people won't recognize? I'm glad you asked. You must master the Art of Familiarity.

Virtual Referrals

There is nothing better than a warm referral from a trusted source. Every salesman knows this and every salesman makes these leads a priority.

The next best thing to a warm referral is a "Virtual Referral." This is a referral that *feels* warm when you call. The Art of Familiarity is about creating virtual referrals. That way, when your salesperson calls the lead the lead will feel *as if* the salesperson was referred by a trusted friend. Remember, the Trade Show Samurai honors sales so we want to provide the best possible lead to our sales team.

There are five basic steps in creating a Virtual Referral:

1.   Plant the Seed
2.   Capture the Lead
3.   Solidify Your Brand
4.   Cultivate Prospects
5.   Harvest the Sales

Plant the Seed

The first step in creating familiarity begins before the show starts. It is your pre-show marketing program and it's quite simple: send a postcard with a photo or image of your booth.

Most unsolicited direct mail goes right in the trash and this postcard will too. However, before it gets tossed, the recipient will glance at it to make sure it is trash. He or she may not even register what it is, but in that tiny little split second you will have made all the impression you need to spark some familiarity when they walk by your booth at the show. "Hmm....," they will think in the back of their mind, "this looks familiar." Then they will see your smiling face and their apprehension will melt away.

Don't overthink this. It is a basic tactic designed for one thing- to spark familiarity.

You can spend all sorts of money sending mail about your products and contests, but a simple postcard with a photo of your booth will suffice.

Capture the Lead

In order to have a Virtual Referral you must pass off the right information to your sales team. Lucky for you, I have included an entire chapter about Lead Cards & Data Collection right after this chapter.

Solidify Your Brand

After your prospect has left your booth, having gone through all four of the Trade Show Samurai Arts, you will want to make sure that they don't forget about you. When your salesperson calls you want to make sure they remember your company. Solidifying your brand means you need to get your company name and logo in front of them—often.

Sponsorships

Trade Show companies want you to be successful. If you are successful, they will be successful. It is for this reason that they offer a virtual smorgasbord of pre-show, during-show and post-show marketing programs for your indulgence.

The marquee sponsors often get the most exposure with their logo and message plastered on signs, lanyards, programs and anything else that will sit still long enough to be printed upon.

Many of these marketing programs are great ways to build familiarity—if you have the money.

If you can't afford to sponsor the show materials or a special event there are still ways to solidify your brand among exhibitors *without* breaking the bank. I call them "Flags".

Flags

"Flags" are constant reminders of your company's existence. A Flag must be visible and frequent. For instance, you could stick up a million flyers around the exhibit hall. Unfortunately, you will risk getting busted by the trade show police because putting up fliers is against the rules at most trades shows.

The trick to creating a good Flag is to let it have the visibility of flyers, without breaking trade show rules.

The Water Bottle Trick

As a Trade Show Samurai you would never leave an unsightly bottle of water sitting out, visible, in your booth. However, until this book sweeps the nation, there aren't very many of us out there. Most trade show exhibitors won't think twice about leaving a bottle of water on the counter. You can use this to your advantage.

Purchase several hundred disposable bottles of water with your company logo (nice and big). These items are not for you, nor are they for attendees. *They are for other exhibitors.*

Before the show opens walk around the show floor introducing yourself to the other exhibitors and offering them a bottle of water or two or three or however many they will need for their thirsty staff. Many of them will drink from them throughout the show leaving them in full view of other attendees.

Voila! The attendees will now see your logo and company name *everywhere* as a constant reminder of your existence! Plus, you get the added benefit of being the nice guy and sharing generously with your fellow exhibitors. It's a win, win, win!

Yinyangle

Several years ago I came up with another great way (if I do say so myself) of planting flags all over the trade show floor. It's a game called "Yinyangle." A Yin-Yang is two matched parts, the game piece dangles from your shirt or lanyard and it sounds Asian fitting perfectly with my Samurai theme—hence the name.

The game consists of paper cards, with your name and logo, and a serial number. The card is clipped to a lanyard worn by the attendee in full view of other attendees.

When one Yinyangle-bearing attendee sees a fellow Yinyangle-bearing attendee on the show floor they stop, introduce themselves and see if their serial numbers match. If they do match the two of them can return to your booth and win a prize!

This is a great game because it's cheap, fun, encourages networking and it gets your logo all over the show floor. Yinyangle is perfect for solidifying your brand at the show.

Visit the Virtual Dojo at TradeShowSamurai.com to learn more about Yinyangle and find some good bottled water vendors.

Uniforms

There are few battles fought by the Trade Show Samurai that cause more angst than what to wear. It is for this reason that booth uniforms—if they are worn at all— generally resort to the lowest common denominator which consists of a logoed golf shirt and tan pants.

The Trade Show Samurai, however, realizes that this sort of "show camouflage" does virtually nothing to help leave a lasting impression on a prospect.

If you're trying to solidify your brand, you should look at uniforms as an important part of the strategy.

Good uniforms look great in their natural setting, but perhaps a bit awkward outside of their natural setting. In other words, you notice when someone wearing a uniform is out of place. Take a football uniform, for instance. A person wearing a football uniform on a football field looks great. They look like a member of the team; they look like they are ready for action and they look like they are in it to win it. Contrast this with a person wearing a football uniform on a subway train...get the picture?

What is important to note, however, is that the person with the football uniform is leaving an important brand message no matter where he or she happens to be whether they are on the field, on the subway or walking down the street. Sure, they may look a little out of place sitting in a restaurant, but you will certainly remember them.

Wear a uniform like this. In the booth the uniform makes you look like part of the team, outside the booth you look like you are supporting your team.

One of the best uniforms I've worn was a while mechanic-style shirt with a huge company logo embroidered on the back, another logo was embroidered on the front along with my name. We all wore matching slacks and bright orange hats. The uniform perfectly coordinated with our booth—it was a sight to see. We looked great collecting the literally thousands of leads while the other booths on our row collected virtually nothing. The uniform was bright, elaborate and garish.

Visit the Virtual Dojo at TradeShowSamurai.com to see a picture of this *epic* uniform.

The moment we stepped out of the booth, however, self-consciousness set in. Even I felt strange walking around the hotel and at parties wearing the uniform. However, it left a great impression. Everyone remembered us by not only our uniforms, but also our actions in the booth. "Hey," they would say, "I remember you guys from the show today. Boy, you were swamped! What was going on over there?"

The right uniform is a powerful Flag. It is a critical part of solidifying your brand. I encourage you to wear something remarkable and to wear it proudly during the show. It is a great, low-cost way to leave a lasting impression.

Alas, the Battle of the Uniform is one of the toughest and most often lost when dealing with the non-Samurai types who is more worried about themselves than a successful show. Be brave my fellow Trade Show Samurai. Ye shall prevail![11]

Cultivate Your Prospects

The nice thing about being a Trade Show Samurai is that you are able to bring home a ton of leads for your sales people. So many, in fact, that they might not have enough time to follow-up with all those leads right away.

You will need to cultivate your prospects so they won't forget about you in spite of all your great work.

You will cultivate them by sending a series of messages to them. Generally this is done through email, but you can use direct mail, Twitter, Facebook or whatever other tool you want.

Enter your leads into your customer database (assuming you have one) and send them a

---

[11] I'm not sure how often the real Samurai used Old English to speak to one another... probably not much.

note right away to thank them for meeting you at the show. Keep it simple and personal, do not use fancy HTML, this should appear to be a personal email from you.

About a week later send another message. A general follow-up message with links to more information about your company would be appropriate, again, keep it simple and personal.

Two weeks later send yet another message. Make it fun. For instance, if you used Yinyangle at the show you might issue a few code numbers that can be redeemed for prizes. You could also do a quiz on your site asking a few questions about your company in return for a small gift. The key here is to be memorable, but not too sales-oriented. Let your salesperson handle the sales later.

Your next message should be about three weeks later. Lastly you can add the list to your regular email list that your company uses on an ongoing basis.

By sending out a series of personal emails to your prospects you will be reinforcing your brand, your company and your products. You will also become familiar to them so when your salesperson finally gets around to calling they will feel as though they were referred by a trusted source—you. This is a virtual referral.

Harvest the Sale

By now you have cultivated the relationship with the prospect so well that when your salesperson calls the prospect the prospect will be open to receiving the call. It is not a cold call, it is a Virtual Referral.

The call will go something like this:

Salesperson	Hi Mr. Smith, I'm Joe Salesguy from Company, Inc. Mike Moyer gave me your name. He said he met you in Boston and you mentioned that you were looking for a new supplier for Worklenukits.
Prospect	*Thinks "Oh yeah, Mike's the guy from that show in Boston. He sent me a few emails. I wish I saved my Yinyangle card, I would have loved to have won those movie tickets.* Hi Joe, thanks for your call. I remember Mike. And yes, my current supplier of Worklenukits has a few quality issues. They often send them with broken Flugeltips and my customers must have working Flugeltips in order to get the full benefit of the product.

Salesperson	I would be happy to get you a quote and a few samples for your engineering department. Mike said you currently use the blue straps, but were interested in learning more about the purple. *From there the salesperson is well on his way to a successful sale. The whole time thinking, "wow, what a great lead!"*

The Art of Familiarity is about building a relationship with prospects. The meeting you have on the show floor is just one step in the relationship building process.

Using a good lead card and following up with prospects are the two most detrimental things companies do during their trade show efforts. The Trade Show Samurai does both.

Chapter Ten

the Lost Art: Lead Cards & Data Collection

I've mentioned the lead card several times before already. You probably have at least a vague understanding of what a lead card is, however, most people have painfully underestimated its importance.

The Samurai Sword

To a Trade Show Samurai the lead card is his or her Samurai Sword. It is the perfect weapon. Creating it takes time, patience and skill just as perfecting its use takes time, patience and skill.

A good lead card is *the single most important tool* in the trade show world. No other tool is more critical to success.

A lead card is where you capture all the qualification data as well as the contact information. It exists in physical form, that is, it is printed on paper or cardstock. When your lead card is perfected it will mirror your conversation and allow you to simply check boxes to capture important data points.

The lead card is one of the first things you and your fellow Trade Show Samurais should put together. It will be a central working document until the very end and will likely go through a number of major changes.

Anatomy of a Lead Card

There are three main sections to a lead card. Contact information, qualifying information and notes. Each section plays an important role in the capture of the qualifiable lead.

Contact Information

The first section is the contact information section. It contains space for typical contact information such as name, address, email address and phone number. In some cases it's useful to record gender or other details. Below is an example for a mock company called Iron Ox. Iron Ox makes chassis for motor homes. In addition to contact information I've also included gender and spouse's name. The vast majority of motor home owners are older married couples. It would not be uncommon for a sales effort to include communication targeted at the man or the woman or both.

About You		
Title: O Mr. O Mrs. O Ms. O Dr.	O M O F	
First Name:	Last Name:	
Spouse:		
E-mail:	Phone Number: ( ) -	
Address:		
City:	State: Zip:	

You rarely have to complete the entire contact information section as people, especially in a professional setting, usually provide a business card that you can staple to the lead sheet. For this reason it is important to have at least one stapler at each data entry kiosk. Notice the above example does not contain a field for a fax number. Motor home owners generally do not have fax machines so collecting this information is unnecessary because it will waste time.

Even if you *do* staple a business card, you have to plan for the possibility that it will fall off. Be sure to at least write the person's name and phone number. That way if it does fall off you can match it back to the lead card later. Also, if you lose it completely you can still contact the person via phone.

Business cards generally don't have spouse information and gender so in the Iron Ox example it is important to complete those fields as well. In this particular example our made-up Trade Show Samurai won't be getting a lot of business cards at all.

Qualifying Information

The next section is qualifying information. This section contains the answer fields to the questions you will ask during the Art of Inquiry. Every question you ask will have a corresponding answer field. If you are asking questions that don't uncover qualifying information you are *wasting time*.

About Your RV					
Status: O New Owner (0-3 mo) O Own (3 mo +) O Shopping (0-6 mo) O Looking (6 mo +)					
Type: O Class A Diesel O Class A Gas O Class C O 5th Wheel O Trailer					
Chassis: O IronOx O Freightliner O Spartan O Ford O Workhorse O Other					
Year: Date Purchased: O New O Used					
Manufacturer:					
Model:					
Average Miles Per Year: O 5K-10K O 10K-20K O 20K-40K O 40K-80K O 80K+					
Average Nights Per Year: O 0-20 O 20-50 O 50-100 O 100-200 O 200+ O Full-time					

All the questions will help rank-order the lead by relative value. Note that this particular lead card will capture information relevant to owners and to non-owners. If the lead card indicates the attendee is an owner the details of the other questions are assumed to pertain to the Current owned chassis. If the lead card indicates a non-owner it is assumed that the rest of the information is with regard to purchase intent.

The information on the lead card will not only allow you to rank-order them for the sales group, but it will give the sales person everything they need to start a meaningful conversation with the individual.

What would the sales person have to do if all you gave her was a business card? This is a typical scenario. The sales person receives a fishbowl filled with business cards from people hoping to win an iPod or something. They would have no idea where to start. They would essentially be cold-calling a list of people who may or may not be interested in buying a motor home. Granted, at least they *might* be interested in the motor home topic, but other than that they have nothing.

Let's say that Iron Ox sells chassis for Class A Diesel motor homes. These are the big, bus-like motor homes with the engines in the back. Who would you, as a salesperson, rather call?

> **Prospect A:** the owner of a used trailer who has owned it for 15 years and uses it two nights per year.

> **Prospect B:** a couple shopping for a new Class A Diesel motor home with a special interest in Iron Ox. They are considering two models from two different manufacturers. Both manufacturers offer Iron Ox chassis, but only one of the models comes standard with Iron Ox. They expect to put about 20,000 miles per year because they are on the road about six months a year.

> **Prospect C:** Larry Jones (555) 673-3203

Prospect C came out of a fishbowl. If you received prospect C from your marketing department you can consider yourself lucky you got anything at all. Prospects A and B came from Trade Show Samurais. Clearly you will spend the most time with prospect B. If, after you close the sale, you have time, you can call prospect A to see if you can upgrade his trailer to a $350,000 Class A diesel motor home.

All the information the sales people need to prioritize their time is available on the lead card.

Notes

The last section is for notes. Notes are relatively useless when it comes to rank-ordering prospects. Additionally, they are difficult to capture and process electronically. If at all possible avoid taking notes.

Notes

The note section, however, serves two purposes. First, it uses up space at the bottom of the card so the card doesn't appear to be wasting paper and makes your lead card look nice. This seems petty and for the most part, it is. However, you will occasionally run up against a subversive-type who will accuse you of being environmentally reckless for using so much paper.

The more important reason for the notes section is to pass off information to *Ninjas*. Ninjas usually won't receive a rank-ordered list of leads; they will receive a stack of lead cards with some good notes about the person who wants to speak with them. It is usually *not* worth it to create a separate lead system to handle press contacts, for instance. At any given show you may capture thousands of prospects but only a small handful of press contacts. The Press Ninja can work directly from the cards.

When you do take notes be as thorough as you can. Complete the contact information as completely as possible and write neatly. When you are in the heat of battle you may not be thinking of handwriting. If you do everything right you will still be wasting your time if your sales team can't read your handwriting!

The entire Lead Card should fit neatly on a 8.5" x 11" piece of paper. Two-sided or multi-page lead cards are not acceptable. They are difficult to use and a waste of time.

Iron Ox Lead Card
RV Trade Show Amendes

About You			
Title: O Mr. O Mrs. O Ms. O Dr.		O M O F	
First Name:		Last Name:	
Spouse:			
E-mail:		Phone Number ( ) -	
Address:			
City:		State: Zip:	

About Your RV

Status: O New Owner (0-1 mo) O Own (3 mo +) O Shopping (0-6 mo) O Looking (6 mo +)

Type: O Class A Diesel O Class A Gas O Class C O 5th Wheel O Trailer

Chassis: O IronOx O Freightliner O Spartan O Ford O Workhorse O Other

Year: Date Purchased: O New O Used

Manufacturer:

Model:

Average Miles Per Year: O 5K-10K O 10K-20K O 20K-40K O 40K-60K O 60K+

Average Nights Per Year: O 0-20 O 20-60 O 60-100 O 100-200 O 200+ O Full-time

Notes

In some cases you will be able to use the same card for multiple attendee types. The above card is fine for motor home owners, prospects as well as valuable Time Bandits that need to be redirected to Ninjas.

However, sometimes you will have to develop a different lead card altogether. For instance, let's pretend that Iron Ox also sells chassis for commercial trucks. The information would look quite different. The lead would be a business and not a couple of retirees. Also, it wouldn't have anything to do with motor homes, although you may see some of the same competitors on the list.

Here is an example of the contact information section on a commercial Iron Ox lead:

About You				
Title: O Mr. O Mrs. O Ms. O Dr.		O M O F		
First Name:		Last Name:		
Company Name:				
Vocation: O Bakery O Laundry O Utility		O Delivery O Other _____		
E-mail:		Phone Number: ( ) -		
Address:				
City:		State: Zip:		

Note that "spouse" is no longer there and that a "Vocation" field has been added. This helps round-round out the business' basic demographics.

The qualification information is also quite different:

About Your Current Truck(s)			
Status: O New Owner (0-3 mo) O Own (3 mo. +) O Shopping (0-6 mo) O Looking (6 mo +)			
Type: O Step-Van O Cutaway O Van O Minivan O Other _____			
Chassis: O Iron Ox O Ford O Chevy O Workhorse O Other _____			
Year: Date Purchased: O New O Used			
Manufacturer:			
Model:			
Average Stops per Day: O 5-10 O 10-20 O 20-40 O 40-80 O 80+			
Number of trucks in Fleet: O 0-20 O 20-50 O 50-100 O 100-200 O 200+			

The information collected is important in terms of being able to rank-order the leads. For instance, fleet size would be an important factor in determining value. Fleet size alone, however, may not be the most important factor. "Stops per Day" gives insight into how the truck is used.

It is important to note that you will not be using two different cards at the same show. Your lead card should capture all possible attendee types at the show. In the above examples the first one was for a consumer show and the second one was for a dealer show.

Checking the Boxes

Notice that nearly all the responses require a simple check of the box. The more often you can create check-box qualification fields the easier your life will be. In some cases there are far too many options to include them all on the lead card. Year, for instance, is a fairly straightforward answer that doesn't require a complete list of all possible years. Manufacturer is another. There may be 10-15 different body manufacturers. In these cases you can have a more comprehensive list in the electronic version of the lead card.

Visit the Virtual Dojo at TradeShowSamurai.com to download an editable Lead Card template.

Beyond the Booth

A good lead card should be the basis of a company's entire lead-generation effort. All lead-generating marketing tactics should be based on the lead-card information. This includes telemarketing leads, internet leads, magazine leads, direct mail leads—everything. The same scoring model should be applied to them all and optimized over time.

This is smart business. It not only creates the best possible lead-filtering available, but also provides a standardize basis for comparing lead sources.

The Trade Show Samurai Getting Pumped-Up

Chapter Eleven

the Dojo

The place where the Trade Show Samurai practices his art is their Dojo, commonly known as the trade show booth or exhibit.

There are a lot of books out there about coordinating a booth or choosing the right conference. If you haven't already figured it out, this is not one of those books. I have two big assumptions. The first is that you have already chosen a show and the second is that you have already figured out how to get your booth there.

For the most part, if you already have a trade show booth, you can probably continue to use it. These days a lot of the companies I see at shows have a pretty spectacular installation. In most cases a few minor tweaks will allow you to "Samuraize" your booth so that it is suitable for a Samurai-style strategy.

Samuraizing the Booth

A good trade show booth has everything it needs and nothing it doesn't. Contrary to popular belief, booths, by themselves do not generate interest and they do not generate traffic. *You* will generate interest in your company and *you* will draw the show traffic into your booth. In the trade show world traffic begets traffic. The more you and your fellow Trade Show Samurais engage attendees the more of them will flock towards your booth. I don't care what it looks like. Given the choice between a cheap booth with a good Trade Show Samurai and a beautiful booth with a typical trade show exhibitor, I'd take the Trade Show Samurai any day of the week. A good Samurai with a little 10' x 10' pop-up booth in the back corner can outperform a typical booth five times the size without the Samurai.

That being said, it's still nice to have a big beautiful booth. But always remember, the purpose of the booth is to make you, the Trade Show Samurai, look good and to let people know that your company has its act together.

The booth is essentially a stage set. It will help set the tone, mood and energy level of the experience for the attendee. If your company has a solid brand vision, it should shine through in your booth. If it does not have a solid brand vision, get one.

As a Trade Show Samurai I like to practice the Art of Frugality (more later). Therefore I opt for a basic booth with bold graphics as a backdrop to me and my team. Try and confine graphic images to those that won't change from year to year. Product images or web site screen shots, for instance, make bad booth graphics because they will need to be redone for the next show. Stick with company colors and logos.

Avoid words like "quality," "service," and "trust," these are meaningless. Most words on a trade show booth, besides the company name and possibly the tag line, are distractions at best. If your booth already has this kind of thing, don't worry about it. You can fix it later. For now, concentrate on the skills of a Trade Show Samurai.

No matter what your booth looks like, make sure you have enough data collection kiosks and that you can arrange the booth equipment to maximize the booth's Coastline.

Maximizing Coastline

The booth's "Coastline" is the unobstructed outer edge of the booth perimeter where the booth's carpet meets the exhibit hall's carpet. It is this line that you will straddle when you assume Trade Show Samurai Stance (one foot on your booth's carpet and one foot on the aisle).

You will want to have about 1.5 Trade Show Samurais for every ten feet of unobstructed Coastline. To prevent human vivisection, simply round up to the nearest Samurai. So, if you have a 10' x 20' booth and only the front 20 feet is unobstructed, you will need three Trade Show Samurais to properly staff it.

An *obstructed* Coastline is one that can't easily be accessed because it is blocked by another exhibit or part of your own booth. Once in a while I'll see a booth that has exterior walls. This is rarely a good strategy unless secrecy and/or exclusivity are part of your brand strategy.

It is important to keep Coastline in mind when choosing the right location for your booth. The more sides of your booth you have exposed, the more Coastline you will have. A 10' x 20' booth will accommodate only three Trade Show Samurais if it is in-line with other booths. A corner position will open up another ten feet of Coastline accommodating five Trade Show Samurais. A peninsula position will open up yet another twenty feet and accommodate eight Trade Show Samurais. And, the coveted island position will open up another ten feet and accommodate nine Trade Show Samurais. You will be three times as productive in an island position than an in-line position.

Nine people in a 10' x 20' booth are a lot of people. You will need to minimize the amount of stuff you have in your booth. The first thing to go should be tables and chairs.

Yes, I said it, lose the tables and chairs. For some reason there are few statements that illicit such heated debate at this one. People love their tables and chairs. And for good reason, it is nice to sit at a table with your laptop open. You can quietly check your email and sip coffee while attendees wander by.

By now you fully understand that this is not the way of the Trade Show Samurai. As a Trade Show Samurai you are always active, always alert and always on your feet. Therefore, tables and chairs are the *worst* pieces of furniture you can have in a trade show booth. There are exceptions to every rule, but Trade Show Samurais never sit on their butts at a trade show. It is virtually impossible to kick ass and take names if you are sitting on your ass.

Maximizing Coastline also requires that you minimize the products in your booth. Many companies bring *every* product in their entire line. It is painful to think that every product does not need to go to every show, but unless the product is serving a function in the Trade Show Samurai-style strategy, they should not be there. This is especially true if you have a narrow island booth like the one I mentioned before.

It's okay to have a few representative products on hand. But be sure to have a Product Ninja who can demonstrate the products to prospects. The Trade Show Samurai should not be doing elaborate product demos.

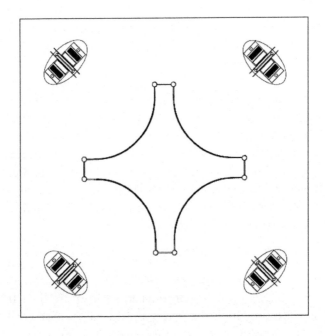

*This 20' x 20' Island with plenty of open Coastline
has eight data-entry kiosks and a center feature that
allows for the neat storage of Trinkets.*

One of my favorite spots is a 20' x 20' island. Such booths are not uncommon and will allow space in the middle storage because Trade Show Samurai will usually be working the Coastline.

Demo Demons

Space isn't the only factor when dealing with products. I also discourage products because they are a major distraction and even a brief conversation about products can kill precious time. For many companies, the trade show is an important milestone in the year. It is the time where they launch new products and services. For this reason it is overwhelmingly tempting to bring your products will you or to [gasp] set up a live demo.

Far too often, however, demo products are in prototype or "beta" form. "Beta" is a codeword for "doesn't work". I can't tell you how many times I've seen a new product on the show floor only to hear things like: "this will be much better for the production version," or, "the production version won't have this smell."

I once knew a company that spent about $50,000 on a prototype for a silly toolbox that attached to the wall. The product was literally *in pieces* before the show even opened! The people who managed that company were pretty dimwitted to begin with, but this move was really short-sighted.

Live software demos are the same. The most common comment is "wow, the Internet sure is slow." Internet connections at conference centers are notorious for behaving badly. Do not rely on them for anything!

There are demons that take over your demos, they hate you and they will bring you down.

The right way to use products in your booth is to first, make them part of your trailer and two, make them talk.

Talking Products

A talking product is one that is designed to help you explain it better to attendees. You can do this by using exploded or cutaway versions of the product and using cards and labels, sometimes called "Silent Salespeople" to highlight specific features that you want to concentrate on. For instance, let's say you are a gun case manufacturer with a new waterproof gun case. Cut the case in half and use labels to call-out the inner workings of the case like the seal, the latch and the compartments. This makes the product talk in that is it now part of the conversation instead of just being a prop.

Iron Ox chassis, for instance, may be tempted to bring some chassis with them. This is very expensive. They should take care to call out the features that are most important. Using cutaway parts and labels will help the Trade Show Samurai walk the attendee through the sales trailer and keep on track. The conversation will stay structured and you can avoid "getting into it" with the attendee. The power of the trailer is that it is specific and concise. Talking products help keep the conversation that way.

You can also use talking groups of products. For instance, I once did some work for a company that manufactured fishing tackle boxes. I implemented a point-of-sale program that increased sales by over 100%. I also reorganized their product line and updated the overall look to be more consistent. Now the products could be displayed as different groups and card and labels could be used to highlight the value of the group of products as opposed to individual features. This called attention to the retail business strategy behind the product line and how the retailers (attendees) could appeal to different groups of buyers.

Busy Bodies

I said before that booth traffic begets booth traffic. It is not uncommon for even the best Trade Show Samurai-run booth to start getting backed-up with attendees who are milling around trying to see what all the activity is about. Many attendees won't have the patience to wait to speak with you. And, finding no easy access to Trinkets, they will depart.

Talking products can help keep them around. Your booth turns into a little museum of interesting facts that can hold an attendees attention for a good five to ten minutes which is plenty of time to get to them. *Keep the bodies busy in your booth*, even when they aren't speaking to you, it will serve you well.

Videos

Instead of having live demos of your products which are time consuming and doomed to failure, you should have a looping three to four minute video showing the important aspects of your product in general terms.

For an even better effect, get a few users and customers on film talking about how awesome you are. Get as many video testimonials as possible and do a continuous loop. Sprinkle in testimonials from different types of users. These short videos will keep your backlog in the booth long enough for you to get to them.

A video can be set up using an external monitor on the data collection kiosk. You can be typing away on one side of the kiosk and attendees can be watching a video on the other side. This saves on equipment costs and keeps the attendees close by.

Visit the Virtual Dojo at TradeShowSamurai.com to see some sample kiosk videos.

Kiosks

By now you've heard me mention the data collection kiosks many times. These kiosks are an essential part of the Trade Show Samurai-style strategy because they convert the lead data into electronic format so that it can be score and distributed to the sales teams in record time.

Kiosks are tables with just enough room for a laptop and a video monitor if you have one. They will also accommodate a badge-zapper. The electronic lead card is set up on the laptop so you can enter the data as you speak with an attendee. It's nice to have custom kiosks that match your booth, but most conferences will rent tall tables that will serve the same function. You won't need the chairs.

If at all possible, use dedicated laptops for this purpose. Try not to use your personal computer. Never mind the fact that they can be easy targets for theft. It is important to have all the kiosks in good working order. Ask you IT department to test each machine before it leaves and let the Trade Show Samurais carry the kiosk computers with them on the airplane.

As a rule of thumb, you will need one kiosk for every Trade Show Samurai in your booth. If space is an issue, try for at least one kiosk for every ten feet of Coastline in your booth. This will mean that Trade Show Samurais will slightly outnumber the kiosks, but they should be able to take turns.

*This data-entry kiosk has two laptops with
electronic lead cards on both. One the door offers
easy access to Trinkets. One of the laptops could
be swapped out for a video monitor.*

Badge-zappers can be expensive to rent, but
in the grand scheme of things they are worth it. In
rare cases you can have one or two central kiosks.
The Trade Show Samurais would take attendees
over to the kiosk to have their badge scanned or
data entered. This system works best when there is a
need to distribute controlled Trinkets like expensive
product samples or price lists. The attendee would
receive this information after coughing up some
professional information.

**Visit the Virtual Dojo at TradeShowSamurai.com to
download a sample Kiosk application.**

Trinket Management

You will need to bring a basket or box to keep your Trinkets. Trinkets should never be easily accessible by attendees. If it is they will help themselves and keep walking.

When we passed out caps, we kept them in tall baskets next to the kiosks so we could grab them easily. It was awkward for an attendee to help themselves because it was so close to the kiosk.

The ABC's of Booth Etiquette

When it comes to the booth, just remember ABC—*Always Be Cleaning*. The correct time to clean the booth is whenever you get a second. If there is a short lull in booth activity, clean. Clean, clean, clean. Trade Show Samurai's know better than to eat or drink at the booth. Eating and drinking is sloppy and disrespectful to attendees.

I was recently at the Everything Organic Expo in Chicago where I say a couple of booth staffers sitting at the table and chairs eating take-out from *McDonalds*. What could be more inappropriate at an organic foods conference? Clearly these people didn't care about their image.

When a Trade Show Samurai gets hungry or thirsty they good take a quick break for a quick bite—outside of the booth.

Be crazy-clean about the booth. Discard any and all food containers that attendees may have left behind. Bring some Windex wipes and wipe down the video screens and kiosks whenever they get slightly dusty. Remove completed lead cards from the clipboards and put them in a safe, very safe, place. Make sure the staplers have staples. Make sure all the Samurais have lead cards. Make sure everyone looks nice.

You can never be too anal about your booth. All Trade Show Samurais should work together to make sure it looks fresh.

Modular Packaging

While many companies have the "one big show" per year, there may be a smattering of smaller, regional shows that draw a more local audience. The Trade Show Samurai doesn't need much to perform at these shows. A simple, 10' x 10' space is usually pretty inexpensive and a small pop-up booth, clean and simple, can serve as a nice backdrop. Pop-up booths usually come in a storage container that doubles as a kiosk.

Most modern trade show booths are fairly easy to assemble, even large booths. And, while you can hire people to assemble them for you, it can be expensive. I like to assemble my own booth whenever possible. Pop-up designs are nice because they are light and portable and easy to assemble.

If you order a new booth, make sure you ask the trade show company to create something you can build yourself, if possible. Also, be sure to request modular packaging. This means they pack individual components of the booth in separate cases. You can have each kiosk packed in its own case. This is important, even if you spend slightly more money.

With the right design, a large trade show booth can be split up to create two or more smaller booths. If they are packaged by individual component you can run two or more smaller shows with the same equipment as one larger show.

For instance, if each kiosk is packed in its own case you can simply ship the number of kiosks you need. Often, trade show booth companies pack different pieces of different booth components in the same cases to save space. For example, they may pack all the countertops in one box and all the legs in another. You want one set of legs, one countertop and associated hardware in once case.

This comes in handy when you attend the regional shows that don't need the whole booth.

Dojo Nirvana

It is much easier to reach Trade Show Nirvana with the right Dojo. Your booth creates the context within which you will deliver your powerful message. It is your temple. Make it work for you.

The right booth will have plenty of open space and just enough kiosks so that all the bodies are busy. It will be clean all the time and create an inviting environment that reflects the personality of your business.

The rest is up to the Trade Show Samurai.

Chapter Twelve

the Art of Frugality- ROI

It all adds up.

Trade Shows run the risk of being a marketing money pit unlike any other. Costs range from those big lump-sums like the booth, the space and the travel to those little nickel & dime costs like union drayage and supplies. While there are some companies that have a pretty good handle on these costs it is easy to lose track of them. It can be a mess.

Combine the cost of the booth and exhibiting expense with hosting parties, paying for hospitably suites and entertaining would-be clients. The monster grows and grows. I once worked for a company that spent over $300,000 on a hotel room tab (it was before I got there!)

Because lead-generation is so low in most trade show exhibits measuring Return On Investment (ROI) is often a meaningless practice. Consider the ROI formula:

(Total *Profit* from Sales − Total Cost of the Show) ÷ Total Cost of the Show= Return on Investment

This nice thing about this formula, and the reason it is so popular, is that it is the true measure of a trade show's value. Unfortunately, it's nearly impossible to calculate. This is why it's so great. Everyone will agree that it's the right measurement, but nobody will know how to actually get the right numbers together so they can calculate it. So it gets put off until the whole idea becomes moot. This usually takes a year or so and by that time you are busy planning for the next show.

Total Sales is impossible to measure because there are no real leads generated from the show. Salespeople sometimes attribute them to the show, but more often than not they will chalk them up to good networking on their part. Salespeople rarely admit that marketing really helped them out.

Total Cost of the Show is easier to measure but it is often spread over a number of different accounting codes such as exhibit, direct mail, advertising, travel, blah, blah, blah. The marketing department must ask the accounting department to jump through hoops to get a reliable number. Keeping cost tracking in mind for future shows, however, accounting departments can probably assign a project code for allocating show costs across departments.

Because the ROI on a trade show is so nebulous, however, many people think it's the perfect time to go a little nuts with the spending. The team goes ahead and orders the lobster and buys the extra drink and takes a cab, rather than the shuttle. The costs somehow get allocated across and between departments and nobody seems to really be paying attention. The problem is real. I once saw a man order a $150 *appetizer*. Ouch.

Frugality is rarely a consistent component of a trade show mostly because it's so hard to track. However, Trade Show Samurai practice the Art of Frugality at each show and they do it by applying a practical measurement called Cost Per Lead (CPL).

Cost Per Lead

CPL is the right way to measure the effectiveness of your trade show effort because it is much easier to manage than ROI. You still have the problem of measuring costs, but you eliminate the tougher problem of measuring related sales. This doesn't mean that sales aren't important- they are. It means that CPL creates a standard measure that can be understood.

Here is the formula for measuring CPL:

Total Costs ÷ Total Leads = Cost per Lead

This elusive little equation is at the heart of the Trade Show Samurai's existence, but it's rarely calculated or tracked by companies because of what it would reveal. It's a number that is too painful to face for most companies. Calculating this number would be a total embarrassment for most trade show organizers. Too few leads and too many dollars make everyone who participates look bad.

However painful it might be, it is an important measure that should not be overlooked. The mere suggestion that you will be measuring CPL is enough to make people not only rethink what they are spending money on, but also make them more careful about collecting leads.

For traditional style trade show strategies the CPL is obscenely high. Think about it. If I spend $100,000 on the trade show and only come back with two leads, the CPL is $50,000 each. Chances are the leads aren't even qualified, but let's pretend they are qualified. Unless you are selling airplanes or tanks, $50,000 is probably too much to spend. It's painful to even think about it, which is why most people choose not to.

When you think about the show in terms of CPL the painful reality of wasting money sets in because, for the responsible employee, spending $50,000 to get a business card is simply not an option. The only way to concretely justify the cost is to lower the CPL. There are two ways to lower CPL: the first is to increase the number of leads you capture and the second is to lower the cost of the show.

Trade Show Samurai are sensitive to both of these techniques and practice the Art of Frugality. Trade Show Samurai do not waste money.

Visit the Virtual Dojo at TradeShowSamurai.com to download a spreadsheet template to help calculate Cost Per Lead.

More Leads

Most of what this book has covered is how to generate more leads at a trade show. By now you should understand that a lead isn't a lead until it is qualifiable and that a fishbowl of business cards do not a lead make. Trade Show Samurai honor sales and we must respect their time by providing insightful material.

Collecting leads is a good thing and it is the most important part of your trade show effort. When it comes to the Art of Frugality, the Trade Show Samurai understands that every new lead they collect will lower the average CPL for the entire show. Therefore, collecting good, qualifiable leads is my number one priority.

That being said, however, you will reach a point of diminishing returns with lead collection alone. In other words, there is a point at which collecting leads begins to have a minimal impact on CPL.

Think about it. Using the example above, let's say your entire show costs $100,000. After you get your first lead your average CPL is $100,000. When you add your next lead the average CPL is $50,000 an so on. Early on the reduction in Average CPL drops dramatically. However, by the time you get to 100 leads the decreases are smaller. When you reach your 100th lead your average CPL is $1,000. Add one more and your Average CPL drops from $1,000 to $990- a mere $10 drop. The drop in average CPL between your 500th and 501st is about 40 cents.

So there is good news and bad news. The good news is that you have 500 awesome, qualifiable leads that cost about $200 each, the bad news is that it's harder to lower your Average CPL.

Important: this does *not* mean that there is a point at which collecting leads is no longer worthwhile, it simply means that to lower CPL you need to find ways to lower the overall cost of the show.

Divide and Conquer

When considering other ways to reduce the Average CPL you need to consider what pieces of your trade show effort are lead-generating and which are not. For instance, you may be one of those companies who host a customer-appreciation reception. The point of this reception is not to generate leads, but to mingle with customers and thank them for all the money they threw your way over the past year. If this effort is important to your marketing efforts then go for it, but consider it a separate expense. Just because the party is going on at the same time in the same town as your trade show, does not mean it is a lead-generating expense. Divide this out. Similarly, if you have salespeople who travel to the show and sit in client meetings all day you should remove them too. A sales meeting can happen anywhere at any time. Just because it is happening at the show does not make it a lead-generating effort.

Stripping out cost that are not directly related to capturing leads will give you a better understanding of your true CPL. If you isolate other costs you will not over-inflate the CPL.

Please note that this is not just a simple accounting trick to justify the show. In fact, it is quite the opposite. When you divide and conquer you will be building a better understanding of the true value of the show and, if your goal is to collect leads, you will be able to cut any efforts that aren't directly related to that effort.

Earlier I told the story of when I was the vice president of marketing for a company that sold financial market data to trading firms. The company was having a hard time finding new sales opportunities post-9-11 because their sweet spot, day traders, had been dropping like flies.

The company had been exhibiting for over 20 years at the Securities Industry Association conference and they had never been able to attribute any leads or actual sales to the show. The year my team, who were trained as Trade Show Samurai, took over we cut the budget by about 80% and came back with 700 leads for the sales team. We did this by cutting anything that wasn't directly tied to generating leads. This meant we cut the hospitality suite and the big dinner and all the things that we didn't feel were going to move the needle.

Don't get me wrong, parties and drinks and treats may be an important part of the show for your company. But when it comes down to go or no go, you may be able to justify going on a bare bones budget and have a great show. Too many companies cut trade shows from their budget because they are unable to measure the success or assess the value.

Trinkets

As mentioned before, these are great tools during the Art of Disengagement. However, keep in mind that passing out Trinkets introduces a variable cost to your CPL that could eventually cancel out any savings. If the leads cost a few hundred dollars anyway, the additional cost may be negligible. However, keep in mind that most Trinkets wind up in the trash.

Comparing Apples to Apples

When you use CPL as the primary measure for your trade show efforts, you can easily compare the cost of a lead from the show to the cost of a lead through other sources like direct mail, for instance (assuming you know how much it costs). Comparing the CPL of the show to other tactics' CPL will help you better understand the results of the trade show relative to other possible ways to squander your precious marketing dollars.

However, not all apples are created equal. Trade Show Samurai apples tend to be tastier than trade show leads from a mild-mannered citizen. They have more actionable information and there are more of them. As a marketing department your role is lead-generation and lead-generation is usually what people are paying attention to.

Your sales department will let you know how tasty the apples are. If they like them they will let you know. If they don't they will let you know. If they aren't telling you try tracking the lead conversion with some kind of customer relationship management system. You need to make sure you find out what's going on with the leads. If your sales team can't convert the leads you brought home from the show then you should reconsider the show. The techniques work.

How Not to be a Trade Show Samurai

Chapter Thirteen

Your Mission

Now that you have seen the light you can never go back. Setting foot on a trade show floor without applying the Four Core Arts of the Trade Show Samurai is akin to stealing from the company. As far as I can tell, you now have a moral obligation to practice the arts and share them with others.

Your mission is to reach Trade Show Nirvana.

The Flow

You will know you have become a Trade Show Samurai when you feel "the Flow." The Flow occurs when you are in the heat of battle and everything is going your way. You are kicking ass and taking names. Every minute of the show is engaged in active lead collection and you marvel at how many great prospects you are uncovering.

Trade Show Nirvana

Feeling the Flow is your first step towards Trade Show Nirvana which is achieved when all the people staffing your booth are feeling it and living it. It's a great feeling, it's a "Trade Show High," that's not from the free drinks at the after party.

Your mission is to achieve Trade Show Nirvana at every show. This means you must not only practice the core Trade Show Samurai Arts yourself, but also you must become a Trade Show Samurai Sensei.

You: the Trade Show Samurai Sensei

Being a Trade Show Samurai Sensei is being someone who offers real, concrete value to your organization. You will be an important part of the sales process and you are indispensible. You are capturing leads for your sales force and you are training others around you to capture leads as well.

It is not going be easy. The Trade Show Samurai Arts push the limits of conventional thinking. People will push back, ridicule and even threaten your Trade Show Samurai way of life. You must persevere and overcome the obstacles because at the end of the day the method will work and you will shine in the eyes of management.

You Are Not Alone

The world can be a lonely place when you are someone who thinks and acts differently. As a Trade Show Samurai you will face many critics who would like to maintain the status quo so they can cut loose at trade shows, enjoy mini candy bars and not be held accountable.

I hope you can see how this is not acceptable. I hope you can see that no matter who you work for you are obligated to do your best.

You are not alone. There are other Trade Show Samurais out there who have also seen the light and are willing to teach the disciplines. I am one of them.

When you face obstacles or setbacks call me, email me, Twitter me, Facebook me, fax me, or text me. All my contact information can be found at TradeShowSamurai.com.

I will do everything I can to help you succeed and have the best show of your life. I am totally committed to your success.

A good day on the show floor

Conclusion

I want you to succeed. I think trade shows are one of the most wonderful parts of business and marketing and I hate seeing them shrink as companies cut back and pull out of important shows. They reduce their spending because it's hard to show a decent ROI.

If all trade shows were run by Trade Show Samurais the industry would explode past even the best "pre-bubble" shows. The booths would be great. You'd come away with cool stuff and attend great parties.

You can do this. I've seen even the greatest skeptics be turned to see the light. By reading this book you must be someone who knows there is a better way.

I'd wish you good luck, but you won't need it!

the end

About the Author

 **Mike Moyer** is a Trade Show Samurai Master. He spent the last 20 years serving as a senior marketing officer for a variety of companies in a variety of industries executing every conceivable lead-generation tactic under the sun. During his career in marketing he developed a special talent for capturing leads at trade shows.

Prior to becoming a Trade Show Samurai Master, Mike worked with a number of companies ranging from consumer products, to automotive, to fine wine.

Mike has a MS in Integrated Marketing Communication from Northwestern University and an MBA from the University of Chicago. He is a guest lecturer in entrepreneurship at both universities and an Adjunct Professor of Entrepreneurship at Northwestern University.

Mike's personal-selling techniques have influenced other markets as well. He is author of the book *How to Make Colleges Want You* which shows students how to properly position themselves for success in the college admissions process.

Mike lives in Lake Forest, Illinois with his wife and two kids.

Talk to Mike

Please feel free to reach out to me with any questions, comments or concerns. Or, as I promised before, if this wasn't the best trade show advice you have ever received I will happily refund your money.

Email: Mike@TradeShowSamurai.com

Phone: (773) 426-6353

Twitter: @ShowSamurai

Facebook: facebook.com/ShowSamurai

Website: TradeShowSamurai.com

Index

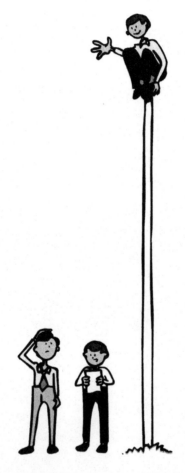

This Trade Show Samurai stuff looks pretty good,
but I'm still going to have to run it up the flagpole for approval.

CPSIA information can be obtained
at www.ICGtesting.com
Printed in the USA
LVOW04s2048250416
485224LV00035B/1648/P